THE WORLD'S CLASSICS

109

THE POEMS OF
GEORGE HERBERT

Oxford University Press, Ely House, London W.1

GLASGOW NEW YORK TORONTO MELBOURNE WELLINGTON
CAPE TOWN SALISBURY IBADAN NAIROBI LUSAKA ADDIS ABABA
BOMBAY CALCUTTA MADRAS KARACHI LAHORE DACCA
KUALA LUMPUR SINGAPORE HONG KONG TOKYO

THE POEMS OF
GEORGE HERBERT

From the text of
F. E. HUTCHINSON

With an Introduction by
HELEN GARDNER

LONDON
OXFORD UNIVERSITY PRESS
New York   Toronto

GEORGE HERBERT

Born, Montgomery, 3 April 1593
Died, Bemerton, Wiltshire, 3 March 1633

George Herbert's The Temple *and* The Church Militant *were first printed in 1633. The other poems were printed mostly post-humously, in various publications. An edition of the poems, based upon that of Dr. A. B. Grosart, was published in* The World's Classics *in 1907 and reprinted in 1912, 1947, and 1952. The present volume, based on* The Works of George Herbert *edited by F. E. Hutchinson for the Oxford English Texts series, and with a new Introduction by Helen Gardner, was first included in* The World's Classics *in 1961 and reprinted in 1964, 1967, and 1969*

Selection and Introduction
© *Oxford University Press 1961*

PRINTED IN GREAT BRITAIN

CONTENTS

CONTENTS

CONTENTS

CONTENTS

CONTENTS

CONTENTS

INTRODUCTION

HERBERT was called by Mr. Aldous Huxley the poet of 'inner weather', our variable English weather. The phrase is an apt one when we think of such poems as 'The Glimpse', or of 'The Flower', where he cries

> How fresh, O Lord, how sweet and clean
> Are thy returns!

wonders that his

>   shrivel'd heart
> Could have recover'd greennesse,

and exclaims

>   It cannot be
>   That I am he
> On whom thy tempests fell all night.

There are many poems like these, that either lament under a cold and clouded sky or rejoice in a burst of sunshine: the two poems called 'The Temper', 'Employment', 'Grace', 'Deniall' (perhaps the most moving of the laments), the fourth of the poems called 'Affliction', 'Gratefulnesse', 'Longing', 'The Search'. They make, perhaps, the most immediate appeal to the modern reader; for today we look in religious poetry for the expression of individual religious experience and respond quickly to what Sir Herbert Read has called 'the true voice of feeling'. Allied to these are poems of revolt and submission, where Herbert kicks against the pricks (the first of the poems called 'Affliction', and 'The Collar'), and others ('The Pearl' or 'The Quip') which seem to carry the echo of old conflicts between the attractions of the world and the call to renounce it.

According to Walton, Herbert on his death-bed sent *The Temple* to his friend Nicholas Ferrar of Little Gidding, with a message telling him that he would find in it 'a picture of the many spiritual Conflicts that have past betwixt God and my Soul, before I could subject mine to the will of Jesus my Master: in whose service I have now found perfect freedom'. And he added: 'If he can think it may turn to the advantage of any dejected poor Soul, let it be made publick: if not, let him burn it: for I and it are less than the least of God's mercies.' It would be naïve to believe that these were Herbert's actual words; but Walton's *Life of Herbert* is founded on good hearsay, and we may well believe that Herbert may have said something not unlike this. It is certain, in any case, that Walton in putting these words into the mouth of the dying Herbert thought them a fitting description of Herbert's book, and that those readers who value *The Temple* primarily as a record of a personal struggle to 'learn Christ' prize it for something it has always been prized for. Throughout the later seventeenth century and the eighteenth, when the kind of poetry Herbert wrote had come to seem old-fashioned, quaint, and even grotesque, *The Temple* continued to be read and loved by Christians of all denominations. The most memorable tribute to it is Richard Baxter's '*Herbert* speaks *to God* like one that *really believeth a God*, and whose business in the world is most *with God*. *Heart-work* and *Heaven-work* make up his Books' and the '*Heart-work*' in *The Temple* made it dear to John Wesley, though he was unable to appreciate its artistry. He adapted, by alterations of metre and style, as many as forty-seven of the poems, and at the end of his life published a selection in their original form. That 'dejected poor Soul' William Cowper, though he thought the poems 'gothick and uncouth', pored over them at the onset of his melancholia and found, if not a cure, an alleviation of his misery.

Herbert died in March 1633 at the age of thirty-nine, and *The Temple* was published later in the same year by the good offices of Nicholas Ferrar. It was close on forty years later that Izaak Walton wrote his *Life of Herbert* (1670), looking back over the great watershed of the Civil War. Walton's art as biographer was to seem 'to use no art at all', and it has received many. In fact, he showed art of the highest order in composing a 'saint's life' for the edification of a later age. His portrait of the young man of good birth and high talent who followed the Court and, when his court hopes were disappointed, retired from the world to become a country parson at Bemerton, has so much of truth and so much of beauty that it would be ungrateful to complain that it tells less than the whole truth. Walton's picture of Herbert's four years at Bemerton, which may be read with Herbert's own book *A Priest to the Temple, or The Country Parson*, gave to the Church of England a legend and an ideal. And Walton's whole picture is given strength as well as grace by his emphasis on Herbert's aristocracy of temper, his exquisite courtesy, and power to win hearts.

But it is a simplification to see Herbert's 'many Conflicts', as Walton does, in terms of a conflict between the attraction of a secular career and the call to take holy orders. It is obvious from the two sonnets that Herbert sent his mother when he was seventeen that religion was throughout the ruling passion of Herbert's life; and it is false, surely, to suggest that such a passion is incompatible with the life of a layman and the holding of high office in the state. The thought of the parable of the talents and the desire to present his 'true account' might well have made a court career seem a real calling to a man of Herbert's birth, breeding, and ability. 'Power to do good is the true and lawful end of aspiring', wrote Francis Bacon, an older friend of Herbert's, and Herbert may well have cherished the idealist's dangerous dream of doing good by winning a place at the source of power. The desire to know that one is serving God, that one is being of use and is not 'an unprofitable servant', is the 'last infirmity' of the religious mind: Herbert calls it 'this deare end . . . my power to serve thee'. The source of the struggles in *The Temple* does not lie in a conflict between the world and a call to serve God at his altar; but in the difficulty of learning to say truly in any calling 'Thy will be done'.

The conflicts of *The Temple* are conflicts with self-will. The pain of the frustration of hopes, in themselves laudable, of the loss of friends and of continual ill health is given its full weight. The deepest pain is the pain of feeling useless, of having nothing to give where so much has been given; and this Herbert knows to be the real nerve-pain of egoism. He knows too what is its cure. If age and sickness take everything, the powers of the mind as well as those of the body, and, most precious, the power to write poetry,

> Yet have they left me, *Thou art still my God.*

If we read *The Temple* primarily as the record of Herbert's love of God and try to find in it the story of a spiritual progress we misread it, or read it back to front. Beautiful and moving as the poems of desolation and of the relief from desolation are they are only a part of the whole. At the beginning, after the didactic 'Church Porch', Herbert sets 'The Altar' and then the long poem 'The Sacrifice'. At the end he sets 'Love'. The arrangement of the poems is not a narrative arrangement, though there are hints of a time sequence in the order in which the poems on the Feasts of the Church occur, and the closing poems on Death, the Day of Judgement, and Heaven give us a sense we have come to a close. But between the opening and the close the connexions from poem to poem are not systematic; they are subtle relations of theme and mood and thought, groups of poems forming variations on the ground theme of the book, the love of God for man. The two poems he wrote on his poetry, both called 'Jordan', announce his theme. In the first he declares he will 'plainly say *My God, My King*'; in the second, recalling Sidney's

'Fool,' said my Muse to me, 'look in thy heart and write',

he hears 'a friend' whisper

> How wide is all this long pretence!
> There is in love a sweetnesse readie penn'd:
> Copie out onely that, and save expense.

: is not only or chiefly the love in his own heart that has
his 'sweetnesse readie penn'd'. He will save his labour by
copying out the love of God as expressed once for all in
Christ Jesus:

> As when the heart says (sighing to be approved)
> O, could I love! and stops: God writeth, Loved.

The firmness with which Herbert in the labyrinth of this
world and of his own feelings holds to the 'silk twist let down
from heav'n' is the source of his peculiar strength as a poet.
His poems are remarkable for clarity of design and precision in
expression. Each, as his editor Dr. Hutchinson has said, 'has
its object well defined'; each moves to a true conclusion,
satisfying to the mind and ear, which, when it arrives, is felt
to have been foreseen from the beginning. Feelings and
thoughts have been refined and controlled by the effort to give
them their aptest expression; and the great variety of verse-forms
Herbert uses is a striking and obvious sign of his desire to
match content perfectly with form. But feeling and thought
had been refined, strengthened, and purified of extravagance
before they received the discipline of poetic expression, by
being brought to the test of their conformity with the truth by
which Herbert lived. The variety of his verse-forms and the
skill with which they are used reminds us that Herbert was
a skilled musician. He is a master of repetition and variation;
but most of all he is a master of the 'full close', finding his
'resting-place' in 'the C Major of this life'.

Some readers have found Herbert too much the artist and
have preferred to his poems with their formal perfections the
more spontaneous, uneven poems of his disciple Henry Vaughan.
Others have found the passion in them too muted when
they are compared with the sonnets of Donne and Hopkins.
Herbert has his own distinctive quality. He has been praised
for 'spiritual stamina' by Mr. T. S. Eliot; he can be praised too
for spiritual subtlety and delicacy. He is remarkable also for

intellectual vivacity; few devotional poets so exercise the mind
and combine the '*Heart-work* and *Heaven-work*' that Baxter
praised with '*Head-work*'. The fineness of his phrasing, the
aptness of his comparisons, the supreme naturalness and ease
of his verse, which, however difficult the stanza used may be,
has the run of good speech, are the product of a fine critical
intelligence that lets nothing by that is inexact or false in tone.
At times he is perhaps over-concise and may puzzle his
readers; at times the emblematic way of thinking, natural in his
age but foreign to ours, may make a poem seem wilfully quaint.
But many of the poems that tease the mind reward its effort,
and some that appear over-ingenious at first sight, such as
'Easter Wings' or 'Trinity Sunday', come on acquaintance to
seem the fruit of a real correspondence between thought,
feeling, and form. But it is not in poems in which we are at
once aware of Herbert's grace of style and wit of thought and
phrasing that the full reward of the intellectual, moral, and
spiritual discipline that lies behind his poetry is given. His
greatest poems are those in which his art enables him, whether
he speaks to us or to his God, to speak in the accent of absolute
sincerity, in the tone of one opening his heart to a friend.

> Ah my deare angrie Lord,
> Since thou dost love, yet strike;
> Cast down, yet help afford;
> Sure I will do the like.
>
> I will complain, yet praise;
> I will bewail, approve:
> And all my sowre-sweet dayes
> I will lament, and love.

HELEN GARDNER

BIBLIOGRAPHICAL NOTE

THE standard edition of *The Works of George Herbert* is by F. E. Hutchinson (Oxford, 1941); this contains an admirable commentary on *The Temple*. Walton's *Life of Herbert* (1670) is reprinted in Walton's *Lives* in The World's Classics. A discussion of Walton's treatment of his material can be found in David Novarr, *The Making of Walton's Lives* (Cornell University Press, 1958). *George Herbert, his Religion and Art*, by Joseph H. Summers (1954), and 'George Herbert and *Caritas*', by Rosemond Tuve (*Journal of the Warburg and Courtauld Institutes*, 1959), combine appreciation of Herbert's art with a just sympathy with his thought, as does *George Herbert* by T. S. Eliot (British Council, Writers and Their Work, no 152, 1962).

THE TEMPLE

The Printers to the Reader

T H E dedication of this work having been made by the
Authour to the *Divine Majestie* onely, how should we now
presume to interest any mortall man in the patronage of it?
Much lesse think we it meet to seek the recommendation of the
Muses, for that which himself was confident to have been in-
spired by a diviner breath then flows from *Helicon*. The world
therefore shall receive it in that naked simplicitie, with which
he left it, without any addition either of support or ornament,
more then is included in it self. We leave it free and unfore-
stalled to every mans judgement, and to the benefit that he
shall finde by perusall. Onely for the clearing of some passages,
we have thought it not unfit to make the common Reader
privie to some few particularities of the condition and disposi-
tion of the Person;

Being nobly born, and as eminently endued with gifts of
the minde, and having by industrie and happy education
perfected them to that great height of excellencie, whereof
his fellowship of Trinitie Colledge in Cambridge, and his
Orator-ship in the Universitie, together with that knowledge
which the Kings Court had taken of him, could make relation
farre above ordinarie. Quitting both his deserts and all the
opportunities that he had for worldly preferment, he betook
himself to the Sanctuarie and Temple of God, choosing rather
to serve at Gods Altar, then to seek the honour of State-em-
ployments. As for those inward enforcements to this course
(for outward there was none) which many of these ensuing
verses bear witnesse of, they detract not from the freedome, but
adde to the honour of this resolution in him. As God had

enabled him, so he accounted him meet not onely to be called, but to be compelled to this service: Wherein his faithfull discharge was such, as may make him justly a companion to the primitive Saints, and a pattern or more for the age he lived in.

To testifie his independencie upon all others, and to quicken his diligence in this kinde, he used in his ordinarie speech, when he made mention of the blessed name of our Lord and Saviour Jesus Christ, to adde, *My Master.*

Next God, he loved that which God himself hath magnified above all things, that is, his Word: so as he hath been heard to make solemne protestation, that he would not part with one leaf thereof for the whole world, if it were offered him in exchange.

His obedience and conformitie to the Church and the discipline thereof was singularly remarkable. Though he abounded in private devotions, yet went he every morning and evening with his familie to the Church; and by his example, exhortations, and encouragements drew the greater part of his parishioners to accompanie him dayly in the publick celebration of Divine Service.

As for worldly matters, his love and esteem to them was so little, as no man can more ambitiously seek, then he did earnestly endeavour the resignation of an Ecclesiasticall dignitie, which he was possessour of. But God permitted not the accomplishment of this desire, having ordained him his instrument for reedifying of the Church belonging thereunto, that had layen ruinated almost twenty yeares. The reparation whereof, having been uneffectually attempted by publick collections, was in the end by his own and some few others private free-will-offerings successfully effected. With the remembrance whereof, as of an especiall good work, when a friend went about to comfort him on his deathbed, he made answer, *It is a good work, if it be sprinkled with the bloud of Christ*: otherwise then in this respect he could finde nothing to glorie or comfort himself with, neither in this, nor in any other thing.

And these are but a few of many that might be said, which
e have chosen to premise as a glance to some parts of the
suing book, and for an example to the Reader. We conclude
l with his own Motto, with which he used to conclude all
ings that might seem to tend any way to his own honour;

Lesse then the least of Gods mercies.

The Dedication

Lord, my first fruits present themselves to thee;
Yet not mine neither: for from thee they came,
And must return. Accept of them and me,
And make us strive, who shall sing best thy name.
Turn their eyes hither, who shall make a gain:
Theirs, who shall hurt themselves or me, refrain.

THE CHURCH-PORCH

Perirrhanterium

I

THOU, whose sweet youth and early hopes inhance
Thy rate and price, and mark thee for a treasure;
Hearken unto a Verser, who may chance
Ryme thee to good, and make a bait of pleasure.
　　A verse may finde him, who a sermon flies,
　　And turn delight into a sacrifice.

2

Beware of lust: it doth pollute and foul
Whom God in Baptisme washt with his own blood.
It blots thy lesson written in thy soul;
The holy lines cannot be understood.
　　How dare those eyes upon a Bible look,
　　Much lesse towards God, whose lust is all their book?

3

Abstain wholly, or wed. Thy bounteous Lord
Allows thee choise of paths: take no by-wayes;
But gladly welcome what he doth afford;
Not grudging, that thy lust hath bounds and staies.
   Continence hath his joy: weigh both; and so
   If rottennesse have more, let Heaven go.

4

If God had laid all common, certainly
Man would have been th' incloser: but since now
God hath impal'd us, on the contrarie
Man breaks the fence, and every ground will plough.
   O what were man, might he himself misplace!
   Sure to be crosse he would shift feet and face.

5

Drink not the third glasse, which thou canst not tame,
When once it is within thee; but before
Mayst rule it, as thou list; and poure the shame,
Which it would poure on thee, upon the floore.
   It is most just to throw that on the ground,
   Which would throw me there, if I keep the round.

6

He that is drunken, may his mother kill
Bigge with his sister: he hath lost the reins,
Is outlawd by himself: all kinde of ill
Did with his liquour slide into his veins.
   The drunkard forfets Man, and doth devest
   All worldly right, save what he hath by beast.

7

Shall I, to please anothers wine-sprung minde,
Lose all mine own? God hath giv'n me a measure

Short of his canne and bodie; must I finde
A pain in that, wherein he findes a pleasure?
    Stay at the third glasse: if thou lose thy hold,
    Then thou art modest, and the wine grows bold.

8

If reason move not Gallants, quit the room,
(All in a shipwrack shift their severall way)
Let not a common ruine thee intombe:
Be not a beast in courtesie; but stay,
    Stay at the third cup, or forgo the place.
    Wine above all things doth Gods stamp deface.

9

Yet, if thou sinne in wine or wantonnesse,
Boast not thereof; nor make thy shame thy glorie.
Frailtie gets pardon by submissivenesse;
But he that boasts, shuts that out of his storie.
    He makes flat warre with God, and doth defie
    With his poore clod of earth the spacious sky.

10

Take not his name, who made thy mouth, in vain:
It gets thee nothing, and hath no excuse.
Lust and wine plead a pleasure, avarice gain:
But the cheap swearer through his open sluce
    Lets his soul runne for nought, as little fearing.
    Were I an *Epicure*, I could bate swearing.

11

When thou dost tell anothers jest, therein
Omit the oathes, which true wit cannot need:
Pick out of tales the mirth, but not the sinne.
He pares his apple, that will cleanly feed.
    Play not away the vertue of that name,
    Which is thy best stake, when griefs make thee tame.

12

The cheapest sinnes most dearely punisht are;
Because to shun them also is so cheap:
For we have wit to mark them, and to spare.
O crumble not away thy souls fair heap.
  If thou wilt die, the gates of hell are broad:
  Pride and full sinnes have made the way a road.

13

Lie not; but let thy heart be true to God,
Thy mouth to it, thy actions to them both:
Cowards tell lies, and those that fear the rod;
The stormie working soul spits lies and froth.
  Dare to be true. Nothing can need a ly:
  A fault, which needs it most, grows two thereby.

14

Flie idlenesse, which yet thou canst not flie
By dressing, mistressing, and complement.
If those take up thy day, the sunne will crie
Against thee: for his light was onely lent.
  God gave thy soul brave wings; put not those feathers
  Into a bed, to sleep out all ill weathers.

15

Art thou a Magistrate? then be severe:
If studious, copie fair, what time hath blurr'd;
Redeem truth from his jawes: if souldier,
Chase brave employments with a naked sword
  Throughout the world. Fool not: for all may have,
  If they dare try, a glorious life, or grave.

16

O England! full of sinne, but most of sloth;
Spit out thy flegme, and fill thy brest with glorie:

Thy Gentrie bleats, as if thy native cloth
Transfus'd a sheepishnesse into thy storie:
    Not that they all are so; but that the most
    Are gone to grasse, and in the pasture lost.

17

This losse springs chiefly from our education.
Some till their ground, but let weeds choke their sonne:
Some mark a partridge, never their childes fashion:
Some ship them over, and the thing is done.
    Studie this art, make it thy great designe;
    And if Gods image move thee not, let thine.

18

Some great estates provide, but doe not breed
A mast'ring minde; so both are lost thereby:
Or els they breed them tender, make them need
All that they leave: this is flat povertie.
    For he, that needs five thousand pound to live,
    Is full as poore as he, that needs but five.

19

The way to make thy sonne rich is to fill
His minde with rest, before his trunk with riches:
For wealth without contentment climbes a hill
To feel those tempests, which fly over ditches.
    But if thy sonne can make ten pound his measure,
    Then all thou addest may be call'd his treasure.

20

When thou dost purpose ought within thy power,
Be sure to doe it, though it be but small:

Constancie knits the bones, and makes us stowre,
When wanton pleasures becken us to thrall.
  Who breaks his own bond, forfeiteth himself:
  What nature made a ship, he makes a shelf.

21

Doe all things like a man, not sneakingly:
Think the king sees thee still; for his King does.
Simpring is but a lay-hypocrisie:
Give it a corner, and the clue undoes.
  Who fears to do ill, sets himself to task:
  Who fears to do well, sure should wear a mask.

22

Look to thy mouth; diseases enter there.
Thou hast two sconces, if thy stomack call;
Carve, or discourse; do not a famine fear.
Who carves, is kind to two; who talks, to all.
  Look on meat, think it dirt, then eat a bit;
  And say withall, Earth to earth I commit.

23

Slight those who say amidst their sickly healths,
Thou liv'st by rule. What doth not so, but man?
Houses are built by rule, and common-wealths.
Entice the trusty sunne, if that thou can,
  From his Ecliptick line: becken the skie.
  Who lives by rule then, keeps good companie.

24

Who keeps no guard upon himself, is slack,
And rots to nothing at the next great thaw.
Man is a shop of rules, a well truss'd pack,
Whose every parcell under-writes a law.
  Lose not thy self, nor give thy humours way:
  God gave them to thee under lock and key.

25

By all means use sometimes to be alone.
Salute thy self: see what thy soul doth wear.
Dare to look in thy chest, for 'tis thine own:
And tumble up and down what thou find'st there.
   Who cannot rest till hee good-fellows finde,
   He breaks up house, turns out of doores his minde.

26

Be thriftie, but not covetous: therefore give
Thy need, thine honour, and thy friend his due.
Never was scraper brave man. Get to live;
Then live, and use it: els, it is not true
   That thou hast gotten. Surely use alone
   Makes money not a contemptible stone.

27

Never exceed thy income. Youth may make
Ev'n with the yeare: but age, if it will hit,
Shoots a bow short, and lessens still his stake,
As the day lessens, and his life with it.
   Thy children, kindred, friends upon thee call;
   Before thy journey fairly part with all.

28

Yet in thy thriving still misdoubt some evil;
Lest gaining gain on thee, and make thee dimme
To all things els. Wealth is the conjurers devil;
Whom when he thinks he hath, the devil hath him.
   Gold thou mayst safely touch; but if it stick
   Unto thy hands, it woundeth to the quick.

29

What skills it, if a bag of stones or gold
About thy neck do drown thee? raise thy head;

Take starres for money; starres not to be told
By any art, yet to be purchased.
   None is so wastefull as the scraping dame.
   She loseth three for one; her soul, rest, fame.

30

By no means runne in debt: take thine own measure.
Who cannot live on twentie pound a yeare,
Cannot on fourtie: he's a man of pleasure,
A kinde of thing that's for it self too deere.
   The curious unthrift makes his clothes too wide,
   And spares himself, but would his taylor chide.

31

Spend not on hopes. They that by pleading clothes
Do fortunes seek, when worth and service fail,
Would have their tale beleeved for their oathes,
And are like empty vessels under sail.
   Old courtiers know this; therefore set out so,
   As all the day thou mayst hold out to go.

32

In clothes, cheap handsomnesse doth bear the bell.
Wisedome's a trimmer thing then shop e're gave.
Say not then, This with that lace will do well;
But, This with my discretion will be brave.
   Much curiousnesse is a perpetuall wooing,
   Nothing with labour, folly long a-doing.

33

Play not for gain, but sport. Who playes for more
Then he can lose with pleasure, stakes his heart;
Perhaps his wives too, and whom she hath bore:
Servants and churches also play their part.
   Onely a herauld, who that way doth passe,
   Findes his crackt name at length in the church-glasse.

34

If yet thou love game at so deere a rate,
Learn this, that hath old gamesters deerely cost:
Dost lose? rise up: dost winne? rise in that state.
Who strive to sit out losing hands, are lost.
   Game is a civil gunpowder, in peace
   Blowing up houses with their whole increase.

35

In conversation boldnesse now bears sway.
But know, that nothing can so foolish be,
As empty boldnesse: therefore first assay
To stuffe thy minde with solid braverie;
   Then march on gallant: get substantiall worth.
   Boldnesse guilds finely, and will set it forth.

36

Be sweet to all. Is thy complexion sowre?
Then keep such companie; make them thy allay:
Get a sharp wife, a servant that will lowre.
A stumbler stumbles least in rugged way.
   Command thy self in chief. He lifes warre knows,
   Whom all his passions follow, as he goes.

37

Catch not at quarrels. He that dares not speak
Plainly and home, is coward of the two.
Think not thy fame at ev'ry twitch will break:
By great deeds shew, that thou canst little do;
   And do them not: that shall thy wisdome be;
   And change thy temperance into braverie.

38

If that thy fame with ev'ry toy be pos'd,
'Tis a thinne webbe, which poysonous fancies make:

But the great souldiers honour was compos'd
Of thicker stuffe, which would endure a shake.
  Wisdome picks friends; civilitie playes the rest.
  A toy shunn'd cleanly passeth with the best.

39

Laugh not too much: the wittie man laughs least:
For wit is newes onely to ignorance.
Lesse at thine own things laugh; lest in the jest
Thy person share, and the conceit advance.
  Make not thy sport, abuses: for the fly
  That feeds on dung, is coloured thereby.

40

Pick out of mirth, like stones out of thy ground,
Profanenesse, filthinesse, abusivenesse.
These are the scumme, with which course wits abound:
The fine may spare these well, yet not go lesse.
  All things are bigge with jest: nothing that's plain,
  But may be wittie, if thou hast the vein.

41

Wit's an unruly engine, wildly striking
Sometimes a friend, sometimes the engineer.
Hast thou the knack? pamper it not with liking:
But if thou want it, buy it not too deere.
  Many, affecting wit beyond their power,
  Have got to be a deare fool for an houre.

42

A sad wise valour is the brave complexion,
That leads the van, and swallows up the cities.
The gigler is a milk-maid, whom infection
Or a fir'd beacon frighteth from his ditties.
  Then he's the sport: the mirth then in him rests,
  And the sad man is cock of all his jests.

43

Towards great persons use respective boldnesse:
That temper gives them theirs, and yet doth take
Nothing from thine: in service, care or coldnesse
Doth ratably thy fortunes marre or make.
   Feed no man in his sinnes: for adulation
   Doth make thee parcell-devil in damnation.

44

Envie not greatnesse: for thou mak'st thereby
Thy self the worse, and so the distance greater.
Be not thine own worm: yet such jealousie,
As hurts not others, but may make thee better,
   Is a good spurre. Correct thy passions spite;
   Then may the beasts draw thee to happy light.

45

When basenesse is exalted, do not bate
The place its honour, for the persons sake.
The shrine is that which thou dost venerate,
And not the beast, that bears it on his back.
   I care not though the cloth of state should be
   Not of rich arras, but mean tapestrie.

46

Thy friend put in thy bosome: wear his eies
Still in thy heart, that he may see what's there.
If cause require, thou art his sacrifice;
Thy drops of bloud must pay down all his fear:
   But love is lost, the way of friendship's gone,
   Though *David* had his *Jonathan*, *Christ* his *John*.

47

Yet be not surety, if thou be a father.
Love is a personall debt. I cannot give

My childrens right, nor ought he take it: rather
Both friends should die, then hinder them to live.
  Fathers first enter bonds to natures ends;
  And are her sureties, ere they are a friends.

48

If thou be single, all thy goods and ground
Submit to love; but yet not more then all.
Give one estate, as one life. None is bound
To work for two, who brought himself to thrall.
  God made me one man; love makes me no more,
  Till labour come, and make my weaknesse score.

49

In thy discourse, if thou desire to please,
All such is courteous, usefull, new, or wittie.
Usefulnesse comes by labour, wit by ease;
Courtesie grows in court; news in the citie.
  Get a good stock of these, then draw the card
  That suites him best, of whom thy speech is heard.

50

Entice all neatly to what they know best;
For so thou dost thy self and him a pleasure:
(But a proud ignorance will lose his rest,
Rather then shew his cards.) Steal from his treasure
  What to ask further. Doubts well rais'd do lock
  The speaker to thee, and preserve thy stock.

51

If thou be Master-gunner, spend not all
That thou canst speak, at once; but husband it,
And give men turns of speech: do not forestall
By lavishnesse thine own, and others wit,
  As if thou mad'st thy will. A civil guest
  Will no more talk all, then eat all the feast.

52

e calm in arguing: for fiercenesse makes
rrour a fault, and truth discourtesie.
Vhy should I feel another mans mistakes
Iore then his sicknesses or povertie?
  In love I should: but anger is not love,
  Nor wisdome neither: therefore gently move.

53

Calmnesse is great advantage: he that lets
Another chafe, may warm him at his fire,
Mark all his wandrings, and enjoy his frets;
As cunning fencers suffer heat to tire.
  Truth dwels not in the clouds: the bow that's there
  Doth often aim at, never hit the sphere.

54

Mark what another sayes: for many are
ull of themselves, and answer their own notion.
Take all into thee; then with equall care
Ballance each dramme of reason, like a potion.
  If truth be with thy friend, be with them both:
  Share in the conquest, and confesse a troth.

55

Be usefull where thou livest, that they may
Both want and wish thy pleasing presence still.
Kindnesse, good parts, great places are the way
To compasse this. Finde out mens wants and will,
  And meet them there. All worldly joyes go lesse
  To the one joy of doing kindnesses.

56

Pitch thy behaviour low, thy projects high;
So shalt thou humble and magnanimous be:

Sink not in spirit: who aimeth at the sky,
Shoots higher much then he that means a tree.
   A grain of glorie mixt with humblenesse
   Cures both a fever and lethargicknesse.

57

Let thy minde still be bent, still plotting where,
And when, and how the businesse may be done.
Slacknesse breeds worms; but the sure traveller,
Though he alight sometimes, still goeth on.
   Active and stirring spirits live alone.
   Write on the others, Here lies such a one.

58

Slight not the smallest losse, whether it be
In love or honour: take account of all;
Shine like the sunne in every corner: see
Whether thy stock of credit swell, or fall.
   Who say, I care not, those I give for lost;
   And to instruct them, will not quit the cost.

59

Scorn no mans love, though of a mean degree;
Love is a present for a mightie king.
Much lesse make any one thy enemie.
As gunnes destroy, so may a little sling.
   The cunning workman never doth refuse
   The meanest tool, that he may chance to use.

60

All forrain wisdome doth amount to this,
To take all that is given; whether wealth,
Or love, or language; nothing comes amisse:
A good digestion turneth all to health:
   And then as farre as fair behaviour may,
   Strike off all scores; none are so cleare as they.

61

Keep all thy native good, and naturalize
All forrain of that name; but scorn their ill:
Embrace their activenesse, not vanities.
Who follows all things, forfeiteth his will.
    If thou observest strangers in each fit,
    In time they'l runne thee out of all thy wit.

62

Affect in things about thee cleanlinesse,
That all may gladly board thee, as a flowre.
Slovens take up their stock of noisomnesse
Beforehand, and anticipate their last houre.
    Let thy mindes sweetnesse have his operation
    Upon thy body, clothes, and habitation.

63

In Almes regard thy means, and others merit.
Think heav'n a better bargain, then to give
Onely thy single market-money for it.
Joyn hands with God to make a man to live.
    Give to all something; to a good poore man,
    Till thou change names, and be where he began.

64

Man is Gods image; but a poore man is
Christs stamp to boot: both images regard.
God reckons for him, counts the favour his:
Write, So much giv'n to God; thou shalt be heard.
    Let thy almes go before, and keep heav'ns gate
    Open for thee; or both may come too late.

65

Restore to God his due in tithe and time:
A tithe purloin'd cankers the whole estate.

Sundaies observe: think when the bells do chime,
'Tis angels musick; therefore come not late.
 God then deals blessings: If a king did so,
 Who would not haste, nay give, to see the show?

66

Twice on the day his due is understood;
For all the week thy food so oft he gave thee.
Thy cheere is mended; bate not of the food,
Because 'tis better, and perhaps may save thee.
 Thwart not the Mighty God: O be not crosse.
 Fast when thou wilt but then, 'tis gain not losse.

67

Though private prayer be a brave designe,
Yet publick hath more promises, more love:
And love's a weight to hearts, to eies a signe.
We all are but cold suitours; let us move
 Where it is warmest. Leave thy six and seven;
 Pray with the most: for where most pray, is heaven.

68

When once thy foot enters the church, be bare.
God is more there, then thou: for thou art there
Onely by his permission. Then beware,
And make thy self all reverence and fear.
 Kneeling ne're spoil'd silk stocking: quit thy state.
 All equall are within the churches gate.

69

Resort to sermons, but to prayers most:
Praying's the end of preaching. O be drest;
Stay not for th' other pin: why, thou hast lost
A joy for it worth worlds. Thus hell doth jest
 Away thy blessings, and extreamly flout thee,
 Thy clothes being fast, but thy soul loose about thee.

70

In time of service seal up both thine eies,
And send them to thine heart; that spying sinne,
They may weep out the stains by them did rise:
Those doores being shut, all by the eare comes in.
  Who marks in church-time others symmetrie,
  Makes all their beautie his deformitie.

71

Let vain or busie thoughts have there no part:
Bring not thy plough, thy plots, thy pleasures thither.
Christ purg'd his temple; so must thou thy heart.
All worldly thoughts are but theeves met together
  To couzin thee. Look to thy actions well:
  For churches are either our heav'n or hell.

72

Judge not the preacher; for he is thy Judge:
If thou mislike him, thou conceiv'st him not.
God calleth preaching folly. Do not grudge
To pick out treasures from an earthen pot.
  The worst speak something good: if all want sense,
  God takes a text, and preacheth patience.

73

He that gets patience, and the blessing which
Preachers conclude with, hath not lost his pains.
He that by being at church escapes the ditch,
Which he might fall in by companions, gains.
  He that loves Gods abode, and to combine
  With saints on earth, shall one day with them shine.

74

Jest not at preachers language, or expression:
How know'st thou, but thy sinnes made him miscarrie?

Then turn thy faults and his into confession:
God sent him, whatsoe're he be: O tarry,
  And love him for his Master: his condition,
  Though it be ill, makes him no ill Physician.

75

None shall in hell such bitter pangs endure,
As those, who mock at Gods way of salvation.
Whom oil and balsames kill, what salve can cure?
They drink with greedinesse a full damnation.
  The Jews refused thunder; and we, folly.
  Though God do hedge us in, yet who is holy?

76

Summe up at night, what thou hast done by day;
And in the morning, what thou hast to do.
Dresse and undresse thy soul: mark the decay
And growth of it: if with thy watch, that too
  Be down, then winde up both; since we shall be
  Most surely judg'd, make thy accounts agree.

77

In brief, acquit thee bravely; play the man.
Look not on pleasures as they come, but go.
Deferre not the least vertue: lifes poore span
Make not an ell, by trifling in thy wo.
  If thou do ill; the joy fades, not the pains:
  If well; the pain doth fade, the joy remains.

SUPERLIMINARE

  THOU, whom the former precepts have
  Sprinkled and taught, how to behave
  Thy self in church; approach, and taste
  The churches mysticall repast.

AVOID, Profanenesse; come not here:
Nothing but holy, pure, and cleare,
Or that which groneth to be so,
May at his perill further go.

THE CHURCH

The Altar — Poem Body Church

A BROKEN ALTAR, Lord, thy servant reares,
Made of a heart, and cemented with teares:
  Whose parts are as thy hand did frame;
  No workmans tool hath touch'd the same.
      A HEART alone
      Is such a stone,
      As nothing but
      Thy pow'r doth cut.
      Wherefore each part
      Of my hard heart
      Meets in this frame,
      To praise thy Name:
  That, if I chance to hold my peace,
  These stones to praise thee may not cease.
O let thy blessed SACRIFICE be mine,
And sanctifie this ALTAR to be thine.

The Sacrifice

Oh all ye, who passe by, whose eyes and minde
To worldly things are sharp, but to me blinde;
To me, who took eyes that I might you finde:
          Was ever grief like mine?

21

The Princes of my people make a head
Against their Maker: they do wish me dead,
Who cannot wish, except I give them bread:
                    Was ever grief like mine?

Without me each one, who doth now me brave,
Had to this day been an Egyptian slave.
They use that power against me, which I gave:
                    Was ever grief, &c.

Mine own Apostle, who the bag did beare,
Though he had all I had, did not forbeare
To sell me also, and to put me there:
                    Was ever grief, &c.

For thirtie pence he did my death devise,
Who at three hundred did the ointment prize,
Not half so sweet as my sweet sacrifice:
                    Was ever grief, &c.

Therefore my soul melts, and my hearts deare treasure
Drops bloud (the onely beads) my words to measure:
O let this cup passe, if it be thy pleasure:
                    Was ever grief, &c.

These drops being temper'd with a sinners tears
A Balsome are for both the Hemispheres:
Curing all wounds, but mine; all, but my fears:
                    Was ever grief, &c.

Yet my Disciples sleep: I cannot gain
One houre of watching; but their drowsie brain
Comforts not me, and doth my doctrine stain:
                    Was ever grief, &c.

Arise, arise, they come. Look how they runne!
Alas! what haste they make to be undone!
How with their lanterns do they seek the sunne!
                    Was ever grief, &c.

With clubs and staves they seek me, as a thief,
Who am the Way and Truth, the true relief;
Most true to those, who are my greatest grief:
     Was ever grief like mine?

Judas, dost thou betray me with a kisse?
Canst thou finde hell about my lips? and misse
Of life, just at the gates of life and blisse?
     Was ever grief, &c.

See, they lay hold on me, not with the hands
Of faith, but furie: yet at their commands
I suffer binding, who have loos'd their bands:
     Was ever grief, &c.

All my Disciples flie; fear puts a barre
Betwixt my friends and me. They leave the starre,
That brought the wise men of the East from farre.
     Was ever grief, &c.

Then from one ruler to another bound
They leade me; urging, that it was not sound
What I taught: Comments would the text confound.
     Was ever grief, &c.

The Priest and rulers all false witness seek
'Gainst him, who seeks not life, but is the meek
And readie Paschal Lambe of this great week:
     Was ever grief, &c.

Then they accuse me of great blasphemie,
That I did thrust into the Deitie,
Who never thought that any robberie:
     Was ever grief, &c.

Some said, that I the Temple to the floore
In three dayes raz'd, and raised as before.
Why, he that built the world can do much more:
     Was ever grief, &c.

Then they condemne me all with that same breath,
Which I do give them daily, unto death.
Thus *Adam* my first breathing rendereth:
                    Was ever grief like mine?

They binde, and leade me unto *Herod*: he
Sends me to *Pilate*. This makes them agree;
But yet their friendship is my enmitie:
                    Was ever grief, &c.

Herod and all his bands do set me light,
Who teach all hands to warre, fingers to fight,
And onely am the Lord of Hosts and might:
                    Was ever grief, &c.

Herod in judgement sits, while I do stand;
Examines me with a censorious hand:
I him obey, who all things else command:
                    Was ever grief, &c.

The *Jews* accuse me with despitefulnesse;
And vying malice with my gentlenesse,
Pick quarrels with their onely happinesse:
                    Was ever grief, &c.

I answer nothing, but with patience prove
If stonie hearts will melt with gentle love.
But who does hawk at eagles with a dove?
                    Was ever grief, &c.

My silence rather doth augment their crie;
My dove doth back into my bosome flie,
Because the raging waters still are high:
                    Was ever grief, &c.

Heark how they crie aloud still, *Crucifie:*
It is not fit he live a day, they crie,
Who cannot live lesse then eternally:
                    Was ever grief, &c.

Pilate, a stranger, holdeth off; but they,
Mine owne deare people, cry, *Away, away*,
With noises confused frighting the day:

> Was ever grief like mine?

Yet still they shout, and crie, and stop their eares,
Putting my life among their sinnes and fears,
And therefore wish *my bloud on them and theirs*:

> Was ever grief, &c.

See how spite cankers things. These words aright
Used, and wished, are the whole worlds light:
But hony is their gall, brightnesse their night:

> Was ever grief, &c.

They choose a murderer, and all agree
In him to do themselves a courtesie:
For it was their own case who killed me:

> Was ever grief, &c.

And a seditious murderer he was:
But I the Prince of peace; peace that doth passe
All understanding, more then heav'n doth glasse:

> Was ever grief, &c.

Why, Cæsar is their onely King, not I:
He clave the stonie rock, when they were drie;
But surely not their hearts, as I well trie:

> Was ever grief, &c.

Ah! how they scourge me! yet my tendernesse
Doubles each lash: and yet their bitternesse
Windes up my grief to a mysteriousnesse:

> Was ever grief, &c.

They buffet him, and box him as they list,
Who grasps the earth and heaven with his fist,
And never yet, whom he would punish, miss'd:

> Was ever grief, &c.

25

Behold, they spit on me in scornfull wise,
Who by my spittle gave the blinde man eies,
Leaving his blindnesse to my enemies:
> Was ever grief like mine?

My face they cover, though it be divine.
As *Moses* face was vailed, so is mine,
Lest on their double-dark souls either shine:
> Was ever grief, &c.

Servants and abjects flout me; they are wittie:
Now prophesie who strikes thee, is their dittie.
So they in me denie themselves all pitie:
> Was ever grief, &c.

And now I am deliver'd unto death,
Which each one calls for so with utmost breath,
That he before me well nigh suffereth:
> Was ever grief, &c.

Weep not, deare friends, since I for both have wept
When all my tears were bloud, the while you slept:
Your tears for your own fortunes should be kept:
> Was ever grief, &c.

The souldiers lead me to the Common Hall;
There they deride me, they abuse me all:
Yet for twelve heav'nly legions I could call:
> Was ever grief, &c.

Then with a scarlet robe they me aray;
Which shews my bloud to be the onely way
And cordiall left to repair mans decay:
> Was ever grief, &c.

Then on my head a crown of thorns I wear:
For these are all the grapes *Sion* doth bear,
Though I my vine planted and watred there:
> Was ever grief, &c.

So sits the earths great curse in *Adams* fall
Upon my head: so I remove it all
From th' earth unto my brows, and bear the thrall:
     Was ever grief like mine?

Then with the reed they gave to me before,
They strike my head, the rock from whence all store
Of heav'nly blessings issue evermore:
     Was ever grief, &c.

They bow their knees to me, and cry, *Hail king*:
What ever scoffes & scornfulnesse can bring,
I am the floore, the sink, where they it fling:
     Was ever grief, &c.

Yet since mans scepters are as frail as reeds,
And thorny all their crowns, bloudie their weeds;
I, who am Truth, turn into truth their deeds:
     Was ever grief, &c.

The souldiers also spit upon that face,
Which Angels did desire to have the grace,
And Prophets, once to see, but found no place:
     Was ever grief, &c.

Thus trimmed, forth they bring me to the rout,
Who *Crucifie him*, crie with one strong shout.
God holds his peace at man, and man cries out:
     Was ever grief, &c.

They leade me in once more, and putting then
Mine own clothes on, they leade me out agen.
Whom devils flie, thus is he toss'd of men:
     Was ever grief, &c.

And now wearie of sport, glad to ingrosse
All spite in one, counting my life their losse,
They carrie me to my most bitter crosse:
     Was ever grief, &c.

My crosse I bear my self, untill I faint:
Then Simon bears it for me by constraint,
The decreed burden of each mortall Saint:
                              Was ever grief like mine?

O all ye who passe by, behold and see;
Man stole the fruit, but I must climbe the tree;
The tree of life to all, but onely me:
                              Was ever grief, &c.

Lo, here I hang, charg'd with a world of sinne,
The greater world o' th' two; for that came in
By words, but this by sorrow I must win:
                              Was ever grief, &c.

Such sorrow as, if sinfull man could feel,
Or feel his part, he would not cease to kneel,
Till all were melted, though he were all steel:
                              Was ever grief, &c.

But, *O my God, my God!* why leav'st thou me,
The sonne, in whom thou dost delight to be?
My God, my God——
                              Never was grief like mine.

Shame tears my soul, my bodie many a wound;
Sharp nails pierce this, but sharper that confound;
Reproches, which are free, while I am bound.
                              Was ever grief, &c.

Now heal thy self, Physician; now come down.
Alas! I did so, when I left my crown
And fathers smile for you, to feel his frown:
                              Was ever grief, &c.

In healing not my self, there doth consist
All that salvation, which ye now resist;
Your safetie in my sicknesse doth subsist:
                              Was ever grief, &c.

Betwixt two theeves I spend my utmost breath,
As he that for some robberie suffereth.
Alas! what have I stollen from you? Death.

                    Was ever grief like mine?

A king my title is, prefixt on high;
Yet by my subjects am condemn'd to die
A servile death in servile companie:

                    Was ever grief, &c.

They give me vineger mingled with gall,
But more with malice: yet, when they did call,
With Manna, Angels food, I fed them all:

                    Was ever grief, &c.

They part my garments, and by lot dispose
My coat, the type of love, which once cur'd those
Who sought for help, never malicious foes:

                    Was ever grief, &c.

Nay, after death their spite shall further go;
For they will pierce my side, I full well know;
That as sinne came, so Sacraments might flow:

                    Was ever grief, &c.

But now I die; now all is finished.
My wo, mans weal: and now I bow my head.
Onely let others say, when I am dead,

                    Never was grief like mine.

The Thanksgiving

OH King of grief! (a title strange, yet true,
    To thee of all kings onely due)
Oh King of wounds! how shall I grieve for thee,
    Who in all grief preventest me?
Shall I weep bloud? why, thou hast wept such store
    That all thy body was one doore.

Shall I be scourged, flouted, boxed, sold?
    'Tis but to tell the tale is told.
My God, my God, why dost thou part from me?
    Was such a grief as cannot be.
Shall I then sing, skipping thy dolefull storie,
    And side with thy triumphant glorie?
Shall thy strokes be my stroking? thorns, my flower?
    Thy rod, my posie? crosse, my bower?
But how then shall I imitate thee, and
    Copie thy fair, though bloudie hand?
Surely I will revenge me on thy love,
    And trie who shall victorious prove.
If thou dost give me wealth, I will restore
    All back unto thee by the poore.
If thou dost give me honour, men shall see,
    The honour doth belong to thee.
I will not marry; or, if she be mine,
    She and her children shall be thine.
My bosome friend, if he blaspheme thy Name,
    I will tear thence his love and fame.
One half of me being gone, the rest I give
    Unto some Chappell, die or live.
As for thy passion—But of that anon,
    When with the other I have done.
For thy predestination I'le contrive,
    That three yeares hence, if I survive,
I'le build a spittle, or mend common wayes,
    But mend mine own without delayes.
Then I will use the works of thy creation,
    As if I us'd them but for fashion.
The world and I will quarrell; and the yeare
    Shall not perceive, that I am here.
My musick shall finde thee, and ev'ry string
    Shall have his attribute to sing;

That all together may accord in thee,
  And prove one God, one harmonie.
If thou shalt give me wit, it shall appeare,
  If thou hast giv'n it me, 'tis here.
Nay, I will reade thy book, and never move
  Till I have found therein thy love,
Thy art of love, which I'le turn back on thee:
  O my deare Saviour, Victorie!
Then for thy passion—I will do for that—
  Alas, my God, I know not what.

The Reprisall

I HAVE consider'd it, and finde
There is no dealing with thy mighty passion:
  For though I die for thee, I am behinde;
    My sinnes deserve the condemnation.

  O make me innocent, that I
May give a disentangled state and free:
  And yet thy wounds still my attempts defie,
    For by thy death I die for thee.

  Ah! was it not enough that thou
By thy eternall glorie didst outgo me?
  Couldst thou not griefs sad conquests me allow,
    But in all vict'ries overthrow me?

  Yet by confession will I come
Into thy conquest: though I can do nought
  Against thee, in thee I will overcome
    The man, who once against thee fought.

The Agonie

PHILOSOPHERS have measur'd mountains,
Fathom'd the depths of seas, of states, and kings,

Walk'd with a staffe to heav'n, and traced fountains:
    But there are two vast, spacious things,
The which to measure it doth more behove:
Yet few there are that sound them; Sinne and Love.

    Who would know Sinne, let him repair
Unto Mount Olivet; there shall he see
A man so wrung with pains, that all his hair,
    His skinne, his garments bloudie be.
Sinne is that presse and vice, which forceth pain
To hunt his cruell food through ev'ry vein.

    Who knows not Love, let him assay
And taste that juice, which on the crosse a pike
Did set again abroach; then let him say
    If ever he did taste the like.
Love is that liquor sweet and most divine,
Which my God feels as bloud; but I, as wine.

The Sinner

LORD, how I am all ague, when I seek
    What I have treasur'd in my memorie!
    Since, if my soul make even with the week,
Each seventh note by right is due to thee.
I finde there quarries of pil'd vanities,
    But shreds of holinesse, that dare not venture
    To shew their face, since crosse to thy decrees:
There the circumference earth is, heav'n the centre.
In so much dregs the quintessence is small:
    The spirit and good extract of my heart
    Comes to about the many hundred part.
Yet Lord restore thine image, heare my call:
    And though my hard heart scarce to thee can grone,
    Remember that thou once didst write in stone.

Good Friday

O MY chief good,
How shall I measure out thy bloud?
How shall I count what thee befell,
    And each grief tell?

    Shall I thy woes
Number according to thy foes?
Or, since one starre show'd thy first breath,
    Shall all thy death?

    Or shall each leaf,
Which falls in Autumne, score a grief?
Or can not leaves, but fruit, be signe
    Of the true vine?

    Then let each houre
Of my whole life one grief devoure;
That thy distresse through all may runne,
    And be my sunne.

    Or rather let
My severall sinnes their sorrows get;
That as each beast his cure doth know,
    Each sinne may so.

SINCE bloud is fittest, Lord, to write
Thy sorrows in, and bloudie fight;
My heart hath store, write there, where in
One box doth lie both ink and sinne:

That when sinne spies so many foes,
Thy whips, thy nails, thy wounds, thy woes,
All come to lodge there, sinne may say,
No room for me, and flie away.

Sinne being gone, oh fill the place,
And keep possession with thy grace;

Lest sinne take courage and return,
And all the writings blot or burn.

Redemption

HAVING been tenant long to a rich Lord,
    Not thriving, I resolved to be bold,
    And make a suit unto him, to afford
A new small rented lease, and cancell th' old.
In heaven at his manour I him sought:
    They told me there, that he was lately gone
    About some land, which he had dearly bought
Long since on earth, to take possession.
I straight return'd, and knowing his great birth,
    Sought him accordingly in great resorts;
    In cities, theatres, gardens, parks, and courts:
At length I heard a ragged noise and mirth
    Of theeves and murderers: there I him espied,
    Who straight, *Your suit is granted*, said, & died.

Sepulchre

O BLESSED bodie! Whither art thou thrown?
No lodging for thee, but a cold hard stone?
So many hearts on earth, and yet not one
                    Receive thee?

Sure there is room within our hearts good store;
For they can lodge transgressions by the score:
Thousands of toyes dwell there, yet out of doore
                    They leave thee.

But that which shews them large, shews them unfit.
What ever sinne did this pure rock commit,
Which holds thee now? Who hath indited it
                    Of murder?

Where our hard hearts have took up stones to brain thee,
And missing this, most falsly did arraigne thee;
Onely these stones in quiet entertain thee,
                    And order.

And as of old the Law by heav'nly art
Was writ in stone; so thou, which also art
The letter of the word, find'st no fit heart
                    To hold thee.

Yet do we still persist as we began,
And so should perish, but that nothing can,
Though it be cold, hard, foul, from loving man
                    Withhold thee.

Easter

RISE heart; thy Lord is risen. Sing his praise
                    Without delayes,
Who takes thee by the hand, that thou likewise
                    With him mayst rise:
That, as his death calcined thee to dust,
His life may make thee gold, and much more, just.

Awake, my lute, and struggle for thy part
                    With all thy art.
The crosse taught all wood to resound his name,
                    Who bore the same.
His stretched sinews taught all strings, what key
Is best to celebrate this most high day.

Consort both heart and lute, and twist a song
                    Pleasant and long:
Or, since all musick is but three parts vied
                    And multiplied,
O let thy blessed Spirit bear a part,
And make up our defects with his sweet art.

I GOT me flowers to straw thy way;
I got me boughs off many a tree:
But thou wast up by break of day,
And brought'st thy sweets along with thee.

The Sunne arising in the East,
Though he give light, & th' East perfume;
If they should offer to contest
With thy arising, they presume.

Can there be any day but this,
Though many sunnes to shine endeavour?
We count three hundred, but we inisse:
There is but one, and that one ever.

Easter-wings

LORD, who createdst man in wealth and store,
   Though foolishly he lost the same,
      Decaying more and more,
        Till he became
         Most poore:
        With thee
       O let me rise
     As larks, harmoniously,
   And sing this day thy victories:
Then shall the fall further the flight in me.

My tender age in sorrow did beginne:
   And still with sicknesses and shame
      Thou didst so punish sinne,
        That I became
         Most thinne.
        With thee
       Let me combine
     And feel this day thy victorie:
   For, if I imp my wing on thine,
Affliction shall advance the flight in me.

H. Baptisme (I)

As he that sees a dark and shadie grove,
    Stayes not, but looks beyond it on the skie;
    So when I view my sinnes, mine eyes remove
More backward still, and to that water flie,
Which is above the heav'ns, whose spring and vent
    Is in my deare Redeemers pierced side.
    O blessed streams! either ye do prevent
And stop our sinnes from growing thick and wide,
Or else give tears to drown them, as they grow.
    In you Redemption measures all my time,
    And spreads the plaister equall to the crime.
You taught the Book of Life my name, that so
    What ever future sinnes should me miscall,
    Your first acquaintance might discredit all.

H. Baptisme (II)

    Since, Lord, to thee
    A narrow way and little gate
Is all the passage, on my infancie
    Thou didst lay hold, and antedate
    My faith in me.

    O let me still
    Write thee great God, and me a childe:
Let me be soft and supple to thy will,
    Small to my self, to others milde,
    Behither ill.

    Although by stealth
    My flesh get on, yet let her sister
My soul bid nothing, but preserve her wealth:
    The growth of flesh is but a blister;
    Childhood is health.

Nature

FULL of rebellion, I would die,
Or fight, or travell, or denie
That thou hast ought to do with me.
O tame my heart;
It is thy highest art
To captivate strong holds to thee.

If thou shalt let this venome lurk,
And in suggestions fume and work,
My soul will turn to bubbles straight,
And thence by kinde
Vanish into a winde,
Making thy workmanship deceit.

O smooth my rugged heart, and there
Engrave thy rev'rend Law and fear;
Or make a new one, since the old
Is saplesse grown,
And a much fitter stone
To hide my dust, then thee to hold.

Sinne (1)

LORD, with what care hast thou begirt us round!
Parents first season us: then schoolmasters
    Deliver us to laws; they send us bound
To rules of reason, holy messengers,
Pulpits and Sundayes, sorrow dogging sinne,
    Afflictions sorted, anguish of all sizes,
    Fine nets and stratagems to catch us in,
Bibles laid open, millions of surprises,
Blessings beforehand, tyes of gratefulnesse,
    The sound of glorie ringing in our eares:
    Without, our shame; within, our consciences;
Angels and grace, eternall hopes and fears.

Yet all these fences and their whole aray
One cunning bosome-sinne blows quite away.

Affliction (1)

WHEN first thou didst entice to thee my heart,
                    I thought the service brave:
So many joyes I writ down for my part,
                    Besides what I might have
Out of my stock of naturall delights,
Augmented with thy gracious benefits.

I looked on thy furniture so fine,
                    And made it fine to me:
Thy glorious houshold-stuffe did me entwine,
                    And 'tice me unto thee.
Such starres I counted mine: both heav'n and earth
Payd me my wages in a world of mirth.

What pleasures could I want, whose King I served,
                    Where joyes my fellows were?
Thus argu'd into hopes, my thoughts reserved
                    No place for grief or fear.
Therefore my sudden soul caught at the place,
And made her youth and fiercenesse seek thy face.

At first thou gav'st me milk and sweetnesses;
                    I had my wish and way:
My dayes were straw'd with flow'rs and happinesse;
                    There was no moneth but May.
But with my yeares sorrow did twist and grow,
And made a partie unawares for wo.

My flesh began unto my soul in pain,
                    Sicknesses cleave my bones;
Consuming agues dwell in ev'ry vein,
                    And tune my breath to grones.

Sorrow was all my soul; I scarce beleeved,
Till grief did tell me roundly, that I lived.

When I got health, thou took'st away my life,
              And more; for my friends die:
My mirth and edge was lost; a blunted knife
              Was of more use then I.
Thus thinne and lean without a fence or friend,
I was blown through with ev'ry storm and winde.

Whereas my birth and spirit rather took
              The way that takes the town;
Thou didst betray me to a lingring book,
              And wrap me in a gown.
I was entangled in the world of strife,
Before I had the power to change my life.

Yet, for I threatned oft the siege to raise,
              Not simpring all mine age,
Thou often didst with Academick praise
              Melt and dissolve my rage.
I took thy sweetned pill, till I came where
I could not go away, nor persevere.

Yet lest perchance I should too happie be
              In my unhappinesse,
Turning my purge to food, thou throwest me
              Into more sicknesses.
Thus doth thy power crosse-bias me, not making
Thine own gift good, yet me from my wayes taking.

Now I am here, what thou wilt do with me
              None of my books will show:
I reade, and sigh, and wish I were a tree;
              For sure then I should grow
To fruit or shade: at least some bird would trust
Her houshold to me, and I should be just.

Yet, though thou troublest me, I must be meek;
     In weaknesse must be stout.
Well, I will change the service, and go seek
     Some other master out.
Ah my deare God! though I am clean forgot,
Let me not love thee, if I love thee not.

Repentance

Lord, I confesse my sinne is great;
 Great is my sinne. Oh! gently treat
With thy quick flow'r, thy momentarie bloom;
     Whose life still pressing
     Is one undressing,
 A steadie aiming at a tombe.

Mans age is two houres work, or three:
 Each day doth round about us see.
Thus are we to delights: but we are all
     To sorrows old,
     If life be told
From what life feeleth, Adams fall.

O let thy height of mercie then
 Compassionate short-breathed men.
Cut me not off for my most foul transgression:
     I do confesse
     My foolishnesse;
 My God, accept of my confession.

Sweeten at length this bitter bowl,
 Which thou hast pour'd into my soul;
Thy wormwood turn to health, windes to fair weather:
     For if thou stay,
     I and this day,
 As we did rise, we die together.

When thou for sinne rebukest man,
Forthwith he waxeth wo and wan:
Bitternesse fills our bowels; all our hearts
               Pine, and decay,
               And drop away,
And carrie with them th' other parts.

But thou wilt sinne and grief destroy;
That so the broken bones may joy,
And tune together in a well-set song,
               Full of his praises,
               Who dead men raises.
Fractures well cur'd make us more strong.

Faith

LORD, how couldst thou so much appease
Thy wrath for sinne as, when mans sight was dimme,
And could see little, to regard his ease,
    And bring by Faith all things to him?

Hungrie I was, and had no meat:
I did conceit a most delicious feast;
I had it straight, and did as truly eat,
    As ever did a welcome guest.

There is a rare outlandish root,
Which when I could not get, I thought it here:
That apprehension cur'd so well my foot,
    That I can walk to heav'n well neare.

I owed thousands and much more:
I did beleeve that I did nothing owe,
And liv'd accordingly; my creditor
    Beleeves so too, and lets me go.

Faith makes me any thing, or all
That I beleeve is in the sacred storie:
And where sinne placeth me in Adams fall,
    Faith sets me higher in his glorie.

If I go lower in the book,
What can be lower then the common manger?
Faith puts me there with him, who sweetly took
    Our flesh and frailtie, death and danger.

If blisse had lien in art or strength,
None but the wise or strong had gained it:
Where now by Faith all arms are of a length;
    One size doth all conditions fit.

A peasant may beleeve as much
As a great Clerk, and reach the highest stature.
Thus dost thou make proud knowledge bend & crouch,
    While grace fills up uneven nature.

When creatures had no reall light
Inherent in them, thou didst make the sunne
Impute a lustre, and allow them bright;
    And in this shew, what Christ hath done.

That which before was darkned clean
With bushie groves, pricking the lookers eie,
Vanisht away, when Faith did change the scene:
    And then appear'd a glorious skie.

What though my bodie runne to dust?
Faith cleaves unto it, counting evr'y grain
With an exact and most particular trust,
    Reserving all for flesh again.

Prayer (1)

PRAYER the Churches banquet, Angels age,
 Gods breath in man returning to his birth,
 The soul in paraphrase, heart in pilgrimage,
The Christian plummet sounding heav'n and earth;
Engine against th' Almightie, sinners towre,
 Reversed thunder, Christ-side-piercing spear,
 The six-daies world transposing in an houre,
A kinde of tune, which all things heare and fear;
Softnesse, and peace, and joy, and love, and blisse,
 Exalted Manna, gladnesse of the best,
 Heaven in ordinarie, man well drest,
The milkie way, the bird of Paradise,
 Church-bels beyond the starres heard, the souls bloud,
 The land of spices; something understood.

The H. Communion

NOT in rich furniture, or fine aray,
 Nor in a wedge of gold,
 Thou, who for me wast sold,
 To me dost now thy self convey;
For so thou should'st without me still have been,
 Leaving within me sinne:

But by the way of nourishment and strength
 Thou creep'st into my breast;
 Making thy way my rest,
 And thy small quantities my length;
Which spread their forces into every part,
 Meeting sinnes force and art.

Yet can these not get over to my soul,
 Leaping the wall that parts

Our souls and fleshy hearts;
But as th' outworks, they may controll
My rebel-flesh, and carrying thy name,
Affright both sinne and shame.

Onely thy grace, which with these elements comes,
Knoweth the ready way,
And hath the privie key,
Op'ning the souls most subtile rooms;
While those to spirits refin'd, at doore attend
Dispatches from their friend.

Give me my captive soul, or take
My bodie also thither.
Another lift like this will make
Them both to be together.

Before that sinne turn'd flesh to stone,
And all our lump to leaven;
A fervent sigh might well have blown
Our innocent earth to heaven.

For sure when Adam did not know
To sinne, or sinne to smother;
He might to heav'n from Paradise go,
As from one room t'another.

Thou hast restor'd us to this ease
By this thy heav'nly bloud;
Which I can go to, when I please,
And leave th' earth to their food.

Antiphon (I)

Cho. Let all the world in ev'ry corner sing,
My God and King.

Vers. The heav'ns are not too high,
His praise may thither flie:

45

The earth is not too low,
His praises there may grow.

Cho. Let all the world in ev'ry corner sing,
My God and King.

Vers. The church with psalms must shout,
No doore can keep them out:
But above all, the heart
Must bear the longest part.

Cho. Let all the world in ev'ry corner sing,
My God and King.

Love I

IMMORTALL Love, authour of this great frame,
Sprung from that beautie which can never fade;
How hath man parcel'd out thy glorious name,
And thrown it on that dust which thou hast made,
While mortall love doth all the title gain!
Which siding with invention, they together
Bear all the sway, possessing heart and brain,
(Thy workmanship) and give thee share in neither.
Wit fancies beautie, beautie raiseth wit:
The world is theirs; they two play out the game,
Thou standing by: and though thy glorious name
Wrought our deliverance from th' infernall pit,
Who sings thy praise? onely a skarf or glove
Doth warm our hands, and make them write of love.

II

IMMORTALL Heat, O let thy greater flame
Attract the lesser to it: let those fires,
Which shall consume the world, first make it tame;
And kindle in our hearts such true desires,

As may consume our lusts, and make thee way.
  Then shall our hearts pant thee; then shall our brain
  All her invention on thine Altar lay,
And there in hymnes send back thy fire again:
Our eies shall see thee, which before saw dust;
  Dust blown by wit, till that they both were blinde:
  Thou shalt recover all thy goods in kinde,
Who wert disseized by usurping lust:
  All knees shall bow to thee; all wits shall rise,
  And praise him who did make and mend our eies.

The Temper (1)

How should I praise thee, Lord! how should my rymes
  Gladly engrave thy love in steel,
  If what my soul doth feel sometimes,
    My soul might ever feel!

Although there were some fourtie heav'ns, or more,
  Sometimes I peere above them all;
  Sometimes I hardly reach a score,
    Sometimes to hell I fall.

O rack me not to such a vast extent;
  Those distances belong to thee:
  The world's too little for thy tent,
    A grave too big for me.

Wilt thou meet arms with man, that thou dost stretch
  A crumme of dust from heav'n to hell?
  Will great God measure with a wretch?
    Shall he thy stature spell?

O let me, when thy roof my soul hath hid,
  O let me roost and nestle there:
  Then of a sinner thou art rid,
    And I of hope and fear.

Yet take thy way; for sure thy way is best:
    Stretch or contract me, thy poore debter:
    This is but tuning of my breast,
      To make the musick better.

Whether I flie with angels, fall with dust,
    Thy hands made both, and I am there:
    Thy power and love, my love and trust
      Make one place ev'ry where.

The Temper (II)

IT cannot be. Where is that mightie joy,
    Which just now took up all my heart?
    Lord, if thou must needs use thy dart,
Save that, and me; or sin for both destroy.

The grosser world stands to thy word and art;
    But thy diviner world of grace
    Thou suddenly dost raise and race,
And ev'ry day a new Creatour art.

O fix thy chair of grace, that all my powers
    May also fix their reverence:
    For when thou dost depart from hence,
They grow unruly, and sit in thy bowers.

Scatter, or binde them all to bend to thee:
    Though elements change, and heaven move,
    Let not thy higher Court remove,
But keep a standing Majestie in me.

Jordan (I)

WHO sayes that fictions onely and false hair
Become a verse? Is there in truth no beautie?
Is all good structure in a winding stair?
May no lines passe, except they do their dutie
    Not to a true, but painted chair?

Is it no verse, except enchanted groves
And sudden arbours shadow course-spunne lines?
Must purling streams refresh a lovers loves?
Must all be vail'd, while he that reades, divines,
    Catching the sense at two removes?

Shepherds are honest people; let them sing:
Riddle who list, for me, and pull for Prime:
I envie no mans nightingale or spring;
Nor let them punish me with losse of rime,
    Who plainly say, *My God, My King.*

Employment (1)

If as a flowre doth spread and die,
    Thou wouldst extend me to some good,
Before I were by frosts extremitie
               Nipt in the bud;

The sweetnesse and the praise were thine;
    But the extension and the room,
Which in thy garland I should fill, were mine
               At thy great doom.

For as thou dost impart thy grace,
    The greater shall our glorie be.
The measure of our joyes is in this place,
               The stuffe with thee.

Let me not languish then, and spend
    A life as barren to thy praise,
As is the dust, to which that life doth tend,
               But with delaies.

All things are busie; onely I
    Neither bring hony with the bees,
Nor flowres to make that, nor the husbandrie
               To water these.

I am no link of thy great chain,
    But all my companie is a weed.
Lord place me in thy consort; give one strain
           To my poore reed.

The H. Scriptures. I

OH Book! infinite sweetnesse! let my heart
    Suck ev'ry letter, and a hony gain,
    Precious for any grief in any part;
To cleare the breast, to mollifie all pain.
Thou art all health, health thriving till it make
    A full eternitie: thou art a masse
    Of strange delights, where we may wish & take.
Ladies, look here; this is the thankfull glasse,
That mends the lookers eyes: this is the well
    That washes what it shows. Who can indeare
    Thy praise too much? thou art heav'ns Lidger here,
Working against the states of death and hell.
    Thou art joyes handsell: heav'n lies flat in thee,
    Subject to ev'ry mounters bended knee.

II

OH that I knew how all thy lights combine,
    And the configurations of their glorie!
    Seeing not onely how each verse doth shine,
But all the constellations of the storie.
This verse marks that, and both do make a motion
    Unto a third, that ten leaves off doth lie:
    Then as dispersed herbs do watch a potion,
These three make up some Christians destinie:

Such are thy secrets, which my life makes good,
    And comments on thee: for in ev'ry thing
    Thy words do finde me out, & parallels bring,
And in another make me understood.
    Starres are poore books, & oftentimes do misse:
    This book of starres lights to eternall blisse.

Whitsunday

LISTEN sweet Dove unto my song,
And spread thy golden wings in me;
Hatching my tender heart so long,
Till it get wing, and flie away with thee.

Where is that fire which once descended
On thy Apostles? thou didst then
Keep open house, richly attended,
Feasting all comers by twelve chosen men.

Such glorious gifts thou didst bestow,
That th' earth did like a heav'n appeare;
The starres were coming down to know
If they might mend their wages, and serve here.

The sunne, which once did shine alone,
Hung down his head, and wisht for night,
When he beheld twelve sunnes for one
Going about the world, and giving light.

But since those pipes of gold, which brought
That cordiall water to our ground,
Were cut and martyr'd by the fault
Of those, who did themselves through their side wound,

Thou shutt'st the doore, and keep'st within;
Scarce a good joy creeps through the chink:
And if the braves of conqu'ring sinne
Did not excite thee, we should wholly sink.

Lord, though we change, thou art the same;
The same sweet God of love and light:
Restore this day, for thy great name,
Unto his ancient and miraculous right.

Grace

My stock lies dead, and no increase
Doth my dull husbandrie improve:
O let thy graces without cease
    Drop from above!

If still the sunne should hide his face,
Thy house would but a dungeon prove,
Thy works nights captives: O let grace
    Drop from above!

The dew doth ev'ry morning fall;
And shall the dew out-strip thy Dove?
The dew, for which grasse cannot call,
    Drop from above.

Death is still working like a mole,
And digs my grave at each remove:
Let grace work too, and on my soul
    Drop from above.

Sinne is still hammering my heart
Unto a hardnesse, void of love:
Let suppling grace, to crosse his art,
    Drop from above.

O come! for thou dost know the way:
Or if to me thou wilt not move,
Remove me, where I need not say,
    Drop from above.

Praise (1)

TO write a verse or two is all the praise,
    That I can raise:
  Mend my estate in any wayes,
    Thou shalt have more.

I go to Church; help me to wings, and I
    Will thither flie;
  Or, if I mount unto the skie,
    I will do more.

Man is all weaknesse; there is no such thing
    As Prince or King:
  His arm is short; yet with a sling
    He may do more.

An herb destill'd, and drunk, may dwell next doore,
    On the same floore,
  To a brave soul: exalt the poore,
    They can do more.

O raise me then! Poore bees, that work all day,
    Sting my delay,
  Who have a work, as well as they,
    And much, much more.

Affliction (II)

    KILL me not ev'ry day,
Thou Lord of life; since thy one death for me
Is more then all my deaths can be,
    Though I in broken pay
Die over each houre of Methusalems stay.

    If all mens tears were let
Into one common sewer, sea, and brine;

What were they all, compar'd to thine?
Wherein if they were set,
They would discolour thy most bloudy sweat.

Thou art my grief alone,
Thou Lord conceal it not: and as thou art
All my delight, so all my smart:
Thy crosse took up in one,
By way of imprest, all my future mone.

Mattens

I CANNOT ope mine eyes,
But thou art ready there to catch
My morning soul and sacrifice:
Then we must needs for that day make a match.

My God, what is a heart?
Silver, or gold, or precious stone,
Or starre, or rainbow, or a part
Of all these things, or all of them in one?

My God, what is a heart,
That thou shouldst it so eye, and wooe,
Powring upon it all thy art,
As if that thou hadst nothing els to do?

Indeed mans whole estate
Amounts (and richly) to serve thee:
He did not heav'n and earth create,
Yet studies them, not him by whom they be.

Teach me thy love to know;
That this new light, which now I see,
May both the work and workman show:
Then by a sunne beam I will climbe to thee.

Sinne (II)

O THAT I could a sinne once see!
We paint the devil foul, yet he
Hath some good in him, all agree.
Sinne is flat opposite to th' Almighty, seeing
It wants the good of *vertue*, and of *being*.

But God more care of us hath had:
If apparitions make us sad,
By sight of sinne we should grow mad.
Yet as in sleep we see foul death, and live:
So devils are our sinnes in perspective.

Even-song

BLEST be the God of love,
Who gave me eyes, and light, and power this day,
Both to be busie, and to play.
But much more blest be God above,
Who gave me sight alone,
Which to himself he did denie:
For when he sees my waies, I dy:
But I have got his sonne, and he hath none.

What have I brought thee home
For this thy love? have I discharg'd the debt,
Which this dayes favour did beget?
I ranne; but all I brought, was fome.
Thy diet, care, and cost
Do end in bubbles, balls of winde;
Of winde to thee whom I have crost,
But balls of wilde-fire to my troubled minde.

Yet still thou goest on,
And now with darknesse closest wearie eyes,
Saying to man, *It doth suffice:
Henceforth repose; your work is done.*

Thus in thy ebony box
Thou dost inclose us, till the day
Put our amendment in our way,
And give new wheels to our disorder'd clocks.

I muse, which shows more love,
The day or night: that is the gale, this th' harbour;
That is the walk, and this the arbour;
Or that the garden, this the grove.
My God, thou art all love.
Not one poore minute scapes thy breast,
But brings a favour from above;
And in this love, more then in bed, I rest.

Church-monuments

WHILE that my soul repairs to her devotion,
Here I intombe my flesh, that it betimes
May take acquaintance of this heap of dust;
To which the blast of deaths incessant motion,
Fed with the exhalation of our crimes,
Drives all at last. Therefore I gladly trust

My bodie to this school, that it may learn
To spell his elements, and finde his birth
Written in dustie heraldrie and lines;
Which dissolution sure doth best discern,
Comparing dust with dust, and earth with earth.
These laugh at Jeat and Marble put for signes,

To sever the good fellowship of dust,
And spoil the meeting. What shall point out them,
When they shall bow, and kneel, and fall down flat
To kisse those heaps, which now they have in trust?
Deare flesh, while I do pray, learn here thy stemme
And true descent; that when thou shalt grow fat,

And wanton in thy cravings, thou mayst know,
That flesh is but the glasse, which holds the dust
That measures all our time; which also shall
Be crumbled into dust. Mark here below
How tame these ashes are, how free from lust,
That thou mayst fit thy self against thy fall.

Church-musick

SWEETEST of sweets, I thank you: when displeasure
  Did through my bodie wound my minde,
You took me thence, and in your house of pleasure
  A daintie lodging me assign'd.

Now I in you without a bodie move,
  Rising and falling with your wings:
We both together sweetly live and love,
  Yet say sometimes, *God help poore Kings.*

Comfort, I'le die; for if you poste from me,
  Sure I shall do so, and much more:
But if I travell in your companie,
  You know the way to heavens doore.

Church-lock and key

I KNOWE it is my sinne, which locks thine eares,
  And bindes thy hands,
Out-crying my requests, drowning my tears;
Or else the chilnesse of my faint demands.

But as cold hands are angrie with the fire,
  And mend it still;
So I do lay the want of my desire,
Not on my sinnes, or coldnesse, but thy will.

Yet heare, O God, onely for his blouds sake
                Which pleads for me:
For though sinnes plead too, yet like stones they make
His blouds sweet current much more loud to be.

The Church-floore

MARK you the floore? that square & speckled stone,
           Which looks so firm and strong,
                Is *Patience*:

And th' other black and grave, wherewith each one
           Is checker'd all along,
                Humilitie:

The gentle rising, which on either hand
           Leads to the Quire above,
                Is *Confidence*:

But the sweet cement, which in one sure band
           Ties the whole frame, is *Love*
                And *Charitie*.

    Hither sometimes Sinne steals, and stains
    The marbles neat and curious veins:
But all is cleansed when the marble weeps.
    Sometimes Death, puffing at the doore,
    Blows all the dust about the floore:
But while he thinks to spoil the room, he sweeps.
    Blest be the *Architect*, whose art
    Could build so strong in a weak heart.

The Windows

LORD, how can man preach thy eternall word?
           He is a brittle crazie glasse:
Yet in thy temple thou dost him afford

This glorious and transcendent place,
To be a window, through thy grace.

But when thou dost anneal in glasse thy storie,
    Making thy life to shine within
The holy Preachers; then the light and glorie
    More rev'rend grows, & more doth win:
        Which else shows watrish, bleak, & thin.

Doctrine and life, colours and light, in one
    When they combine and mingle, bring
A strong regard and aw: but speech alone
    Doth vanish like a flaring thing,
        And in the eare, not conscience ring.

Trinitie Sunday

LORD, who hast form'd me out of mud,
    And hast redeem'd me through thy bloud,
    And sanctifi'd me to do good;

Purge all my sinnes done heretofore:
    For I confesse my heavie score,
    And I will strive to sinne no more.

Enrich my heart, mouth, hands in me,
    With faith, with hope, with charitie;
    That I may runne, rise, rest with thee.

Content

PEACE mutt'ring thoughts, and do not grudge to keep
    Within the walls of your own breast:
Who cannot on his own bed sweetly sleep,
    Can on anothers hardly rest.

Gad not abroad at ev'ry quest and call
   Of an untrained hope or passion.
To court each place or fortune that doth fall,
   Is wantonnesse in contemplation.

Mark how the fire in flints doth quiet lie,
   Content and warm t' it self alone:
But when it would appeare to others eye,
   Without a knock it never shone.

Give me the pliant minde, whose gentle measure
   Complies and suits with all estates;
Which can let loose to a crown, and yet with pleasure
   Take up within a cloisters gates.

This soul doth span the world, and hang content
   From either pole unto the centre:
Where in each room of the well-furnisht tent
   He lies warm, and without adventure.

The brags of life are but a nine dayes wonder;
   And after death the fumes that spring
From private bodies make as big a thunder,
   As those which rise from a huge King.

Onely thy Chronicle is lost; and yet
   Better by worms be all once spent,
Then to have hellish moths still gnaw and fret
   Thy name in books, which may not rent:

When all thy deeds, whose brunt thou feel'st alone,
   Are chaw'd by others pens and tongue;
And as their wit is, their digestion,
   Thy nourisht fame is weak or strong.

Then cease discoursing soul, till thine own ground,
   Do not thy self or friends importune.
He that by seeking hath himself once found,
   Hath ever found a happie fortune.

The Quidditie

My God, a verse is not a crown,
No point of honour, or gay suit,
No hawk, or banquet, or renown,
Nor a good sword, nor yet a lute:

It cannot vault, or dance, or play;
It never was in *France* or *Spain*;
Nor can it entertain the day
With my great stable or demain:

It is no office, art, or news,
Nor the Exchange, or busie Hall;
But it is that which while I use
I am with thee, and *most take all*.

Humilitie

I saw the Vertues sitting hand in hand
In sev'rall ranks upon an azure throne,
Where all the beasts and fowl by their command
Presented tokens of submission.
Humilitie, who sat the lowest there
                    To execute their call,
When by the beasts the presents tendred were,
                    Gave them about to all.

The angrie Lion did present his paw,
Which by consent was giv'n to Mansuetude.
The fearfull Hare her eares, which by their law
Humilitie did reach to Fortitude.
The jealous Turkie brought his corall chain;
                    That went to Temperance.
On Justice was bestow'd the Foxes brain,
                    Kill'd in the way by chance.

At length the Crow bringing the Peacocks plume,
(For he would not) as they beheld the grace
Of that brave gift, each one began to fume,
And challenge it, as proper to his place,
Till they fell out: which when the beasts espied,
                They leapt upon the throne;
And if the Fox had liv'd to rule their side,
                They had depos'd each one.

Humilitie, who held the plume, at this
Did weep so fast, that the tears trickling down
Spoil'd all the train: then saying, *Here it is
For which ye wrangle*, made them turn their frown
Against the beasts: so joyntly bandying,
                They drive them soon away;
And then amerc'd them, double gifts to bring
                At the next Session-day.

Frailtie

LORD, in my silence how do I despise
                What upon trust
Is styled *honour*, *riches*, or *fair eyes*;
                But is *fair dust!*
    I surname them *guilded clay*,
        Deare earth, *fine grasse* or *hay*;
In all, I think my foot doth ever tread
                Upon their head.

But when I view abroad both Regiments;
                The worlds, and thine:
Thine clad with simplenesse, and sad events;
                The other fine,
    Full of glorie and gay weeds,
        Brave language, braver deeds:
That which was dust before, doth quickly rise,
                And prick mine eyes.

O brook not this, lest if what *
   My foot did t.
Affront those joyes, wherewith thou *
    And long since we*
  My poore soul, ev'n sick of love:
   It may a Babel prove
Commodious to conquer heav'n and thee
    Planted in me.

Constancie

  W H O is the honest man?
He that doth still and strongly good pursue,
To God, his neighbour, and himself most true:
  Whom neither force nor fawning can
Unpinne, or wrench from giving all their due.

  Whose honestie is not
So loose or easie, that a ruffling winde
Can blow away, or glittering look it blinde:
  Who rides his sure and even trot,
While the world now rides by, now lags behinde.

  Who, when great trials come,
Nor seeks, nor shunnes them; but doth calmly stay,
Till he the thing and the example weigh:
  All being brought into a summe,
What place or person calls for, he doth pay.

  Whom none can work or wooe
To use in any thing a trick or sleight;
For above all things he abhorres deceit:
  His words and works and fashion too
All of a piece, and all are cleare and straight.

Who never melts or thaws
At close tentations: when the day is done,
His goodnesse sets not, but in dark can runne:
  The sunne to others writeth laws,
And is their vertue; Vertue is his Sunne.

Who, when he is to treat
With sick folks, women, those whom passions sway,
Allows for that, and keeps his constant way:
  Whom others faults do not defeat;
But though men fail him, yet his part doth play.

Whom nothing can procure,
When the wide world runnes bias from his will,
To writhe his limbes, and share, not mend the ill.
  This is the Mark-man, safe and sure,
Who still is right, and prayes to be so still.

Affliction (III)

My heart did heave, and there came forth, *O God!*
By that I knew that thou wast in the grief,
To guide and govern it to my relief,
  Making a scepter of the rod:
   Hadst thou not had thy part,
Sure the unruly sigh had broke my heart.

But since thy breath gave me both life and shape,
Thou knowst my tallies; and when there's assign'd
So much breath to a sigh, what's then behinde?
  Or if some yeares with it escape,
   The sigh then onely is
A gale to bring me sooner to my blisse.

Thy life on earth was grief, and thou art still
Constant unto it, making it to be
A point of honour, now to grieve in me,
    And in thy members suffer ill.
        They who lament one crosse,
Thou dying dayly, praise thee to thy losse.

The Starre

BRIGHT spark, shot from a brighter place,
  Where beams surround my Saviours face,
      Canst thou be any where
      So well as there?

Yet, if thou wilt from thence depart,
  Take a bad lodging in my heart;
      For thou canst make a debter,
      And make it better.

First with thy fire-work burn to dust
  Folly, and worse then folly, lust:
      Then with thy light refine,
      And make it shine:

So disengag'd from sinne and sicknesse,
  Touch it with thy celestiall quicknesse,
      That it may hang and move
      After thy love.

Then with our trinitie of light,
  Motion, and heat, let's take our flight
      Unto the place where thou
      Before didst bow.

Get me a standing there, and place
  Among the beams, which crown the face
      Of him, who dy'd to part
      Sinne and my heart:

That so among the rest I may
  Glitter, and curle, and winde as they:
    That winding is their fashion
      Of adoration.

Sure thou wilt joy, by gaining me
  To flie home like a laden bee
    Unto that hive of beams
      And garland streams.

Sunday

      O DAY most calm, most bright,
The fruit of this, the next worlds bud,
Th' indorsement of supreme delight,
Writ by a friend, and with his bloud;
The couch of time; cares balm and bay:
The week were dark, but for thy light:
      Thy torch doth show the way.

      The other dayes and thou
Make up one man; whose face thou art,
Knocking at heaven with thy brow:
The worky-daies are the back-part;
The burden of the week lies there,
Making the whole to stoup and bow,
      Till thy release appeare.

      Man had straight forward gone
To endlesse death: but thou dost pull
And turn us round to look on one,
Whom, if we were not very dull,
We could not choose but look on still;
Since there is no place so alone,
      The which he doth not fill.

Sundaies the pillars are,
On which heav'ns palace arched lies:
The other dayes fill up the spare
And hollow room with vanities.
They are the fruitfull beds and borders
In Gods rich garden: that is bare,
   Which parts their ranks and orders.

The Sundaies of mans life,
Thredded together on times string,
Make bracelets to adorn the wife
Of the eternall glorious King.
On Sunday heavens gate stands ope;
Blessings are plentifull and rife,
   More plentifull then hope.

This day my Saviour rose,
And did inclose this light for his:
That, as each beast his manger knows,
Man might not of his fodder misse.
Christ hath took in this piece of ground,
And made a garden there for those
   Who want herbs for their wound.

The rest of our Creation
Our great Redeemer did remove
With the same shake, which at his passion
Did th' earth and all things with it move.
As Sampson bore the doores away,
Christs hands, though nail'd, wrought our salvation,
   And did unhinge that day.

The brightnesse of that day
We sullied by our foul offence:
Wherefore that robe we cast away,
Having a new at his expence,

Whose drops of bloud paid the full price,
That was requir'd to make us gay,
    And fit for Paradise.

    Thou art a day of mirth:
And where the week-dayes trail on ground,
Thy flight is higher, as thy birth.
O let me take thee at the bound,
Leaping with thee from sev'n to sev'n,
Till that we both, being toss'd from earth,
    Flie hand in hand to heav'n!

Avarice

MONEY, thou bane of blisse, & sourse of wo,
   Whence com'st thou, that thou art so fresh and fine?
   I know thy parentage is base and low:
Man found thee poore and dirtie in a mine.
   Surely thou didst so little contribute
    To this great kingdome, which thou now hast got,
   That he was fain, when thou wert destitute,
To digge thee out of thy dark cave and grot:
   Then forcing thee by fire he made thee bright:
    Nay, thou hast got the face of man; for we
   Have with our stamp and seal transferr'd our right:
Thou art the man, and man but drosse to thee.
   Man calleth thee his wealth, who made thee rich;
   And while he digs out thee, falls in the ditch.

Ana- $\left\{ \begin{array}{l} \text{MARY} \\ \text{ARMY} \end{array} \right\}$ *gram.*

HOW well her name an *Army* doth present,
In whom the *Lord of Hosts* did pitch his tent!

To all Angels and Saints

OH glorious spirits, who after all your bands
See the smooth face of God without a frown
                    Or strict commands;
Where ev'ry one is king, and hath his crown,
If not upon his head, yet in his hands:

Not out of envie or maliciousnesse
Do I forbear to crave your speciall aid:
                    I would addresse
My vows to thee most gladly, Blessed Maid,
And Mother of my God, in my distresse.

Thou art the holy mine, whence came the gold,
The great restorative for all decay
                    In young and old;
Thou art the cabinet where the jewell lay:
Chiefly to thee would I my soul unfold:

But now, alas, I dare not; for our King,
Whom we do all joyntly adore and praise,
                    Bids no such thing:
And where his pleasure no injunction layes,
('Tis your own case) ye never move a wing.

All worship is prerogative, and a flower
Of his rich crown, from whom lyes no appeal
                    At the last houre:
Therefore we dare not from his garland steal,
To make a posie for inferiour power.

Although then others court you, if ye know
What's done on earth, we shall not fare the worse,
                    Who do not so;
Since we are ever ready to disburse,
If any one our Masters hand can show.

Employment (II)

HE that is weary, let him sit.
>> My soul would stirre
And trade in courtesies and wit,
>> Quitting the furre
To cold complexions needing it.

Man is no starre, but a quick coal
>> Of mortall fire:
Who blows it not, nor doth controll
>> A faint desire,
Lets his own ashes choke his soul.

When th' elements did for place contest
>> With him, whose will
Ordain'd the highest to be best;
>> The earth sat still,
And by the others is opprest.

Life is a businesse, not good cheer;
>> Ever in warres.
The sunne still shineth there or here,
>> Whereas the starres
Watch an advantage to appeare.

Oh that I were an Orenge-tree,
>> That busie plant!
Then should I ever laden be,
>> And never want
Some fruit for him that dressed me.

But we are still too young or old;
>> The Man is gone,
Before we do our wares unfold:
>> So we freeze on,
Untill the grave increase our cold.

Deniall

WHEN my devotions could not pierce
      Thy silent eares;
Then was my heart broken, as was my verse:
    My breast was full of fears
          And disorder:

My bent thoughts, like a brittle bow,
      Did flie asunder:
Each took his way; some would to pleasures go,
    Some to the warres and thunder
          Of alarms.

As good go any where, they say,
      As to benumme
Both knees and heart, in crying night and day,
    Come, come, my God, O come,
          But no hearing.

O that thou shouldst give dust a tongue
      To crie to thee,
And then not heare it crying! all day long
    My heart was in my knee,
          But no hearing.

Therefore my soul lay out of sight,
      Untun'd, unstrung:
My feeble spirit, unable to look right,
    Like a nipt blossome, hung
          Discontented.

O cheer and tune my heartlesse breast,
      Deferre no time;
That so thy favours granting my request,
    They and my minde may chime,
          And mend my ryme.

Christmas

ALL after pleasures as I rid one day,
  My horse and I, both tir'd, bodie and minde,
  With full crie of affections, quite astray,
I took up in the next inne I could finde.
There when I came, whom found I but my deare,
  My dearest Lord, expecting till the grief
  Of pleasures brought me to him, readie there
To be all passengers most sweet relief?
O Thou, whose glorious, yet contracted light,
  Wrapt in nights mantle, stole into a manger;
  Since my dark soul and brutish is thy right,
To Man of all beasts be not thou a stranger:
  Furnish & deck my soul, that thou mayst have
  A better lodging then a rack or grave.

THE shepherds sing; and shall I silent be?
          My God, no hymne for thee?
My soul's a shepherd too; a flock it feeds
          Of thoughts, and words, and deeds.
The pasture is thy word: the streams, thy grace
          Enriching all the place.
Shepherd and flock shall sing, and all my powers
          Out-sing the day-light houres.
Then we will chide the sunne for letting night
          Take up his place and right:
We sing one common Lord; wherefore he should
          Himself the candle hold.
I will go searching, till I finde a sunne
          Shall stay, till we have done;
A willing shiner, that shall shine as gladly,
          As frost-nipt sunnes look sadly.
Then we will sing, and shine all our own day,
          And one another pay:

72

His beams shall cheer my breast, and both so twine,
Till ev'n his beams sing, and my musick shine.

Ungratefulnesse

LORD, with what bountie and rare clemencie
            Hast thou redeem'd us from the grave!
                If thou hadst let us runne,
            Gladly had man ador'd the sunne,
                And thought his god most brave;
Where now we shall be better gods then he.

Thou hast but two rare cabinets full of treasure,
            The *Trinitie*, and *Incarnation*:
                Thou hast unlockt them both,
            And made them jewels to betroth
                The work of thy creation
Unto thy self in everlasting pleasure.

The statelier cabinet is the *Trinitie*,
            Whose sparkling light accesse denies:
                Therefore thou dost not show
            This fully to us, till death blow
                The dust into our eyes:
For by that powder thou wilt make us see.

But all thy sweets are packt up in the other;
            Thy mercies thither flock and flow:
                That as the first affrights,
            This may allure us with delights;
                Because this box we know;
For we have all of us just such another.

But man is close, reserv'd, and dark to thee:
            When thou demandest but a heart,
                He cavils instantly.

In his poore cabinet of bone
　　　Sinnes have their box apart,
Defrauding thee, who gavest two for one.

Sighs and Grones

　　　　　O DO not use me
After my sinnes! look not on my desert,
But on thy glorie! then thou wilt reform
And not refuse me: for thou onely art
The mightie God, but I a sillie worm;
　　　　　O do not bruise me!

　　　　　O do not urge me!
For what account can thy ill steward make?
I have abus'd thy stock, destroy'd thy woods,
Suckt all thy magazens: my head did ake,
Till it found out how to consume thy goods:
　　　　　O do not scourge me!

　　　　　O do not blinde me!
I have deserv'd that an Egyptian night
Should thicken all my powers; because my lust
Hath still sow'd fig-leaves to exclude thy light:
But I am frailtie, and already dust;
　　　　　O do not grinde me!

　　　　　O do not fill me
With the turn'd viall of thy bitter wrath!
For thou hast other vessels full of bloud,
A part whereof my Saviour empti'd hath,
Ev'n unto death: since he di'd for my good,
　　　　　O do not kill me!

　　　　　But O reprieve me!
For thou hast life and death at thy command;

Thou art both *Judge* and *Saviour*, *feast* and *rod*,
Cordiall and *Corrosive*: put not thy hand
Into the bitter box; but O my God,
                 My God, relieve me!

The World

LOVE built a stately house; where *Fortune* came,
And spinning phansies, she was heard to say,
That her fine cobwebs did support the frame,
Whereas they were supported by the same:
But *Wisdome* quickly swept them all away.

Then *Pleasure* came, who, liking not the fashion,
Began to make *Balcones*, *Terraces*,
Till she had weakned all by alteration:
But rev'rend *laws*, and many a *proclamation*
Reformed all at length with menaces.

Then enter'd *Sinne*, and with that Sycomore,
Whose leaves first sheltred man from drought & dew,
Working and winding slily evermore,
The inward walls and sommers cleft and tore:
But *Grace* shor'd these, and cut that as it grew.

Then *Sinne* combin'd with *Death* in a firm band
To raze the building to the very floore:
Which they effected, none could them withstand.
But *Love* and *Grace* took *Glorie* by the hand,
And built a braver Palace then before.

Coloss. 3. 3

Our life is hid with Christ in God

My words & thoughts do both express this notion,
That *Life* hath with the sun a double motion.

The   first   *Is* straight, and our diurnall friend,
The   other   *Hid* and doth obliquely bend.
One life is wrapt *In* flesh, and tends to earth:
The other winds towards *Him*, whose happie birth
Taught me to live here so, *That* still one eye
Should aim and shoot at that which *Is* on high:
Quitting with daily labour all *My* pleasure,
To gain at harvest an eternall   *Treasure*.

Vanitie (1)

THE fleet Astronomer can bore,
And thred the spheres with his quick-piercing minde:
He views their stations, walks from doore to doore,
            Surveys, as if he had design'd
To make a purchase there: he sees their dances,
            And knoweth long before
Both their full-ey'd aspects, and secret glances.

            The nimble Diver with his side
Cuts through the working waves, that he may fetch
His dearely-earned pearl, which God did hide
            On purpose from the ventrous wretch;
That he might save his life, and also hers,
            Who with excessive pride
Her own destruction and his danger wears.

            The subtil Chymick can devest
And strip the creature naked, till he finde
The callow principles within their nest:
            There he imparts to them his minde,
Admitted to their bed-chamber, before
            They appeare trim and drest
To ordinarie suitours at the doore.

What hath not man sought out and found,
But his deare God? who yet his glorious law
Embosomes in us, mellowing the ground
　　　With showres and frosts, with love & aw,
So that we need not say, Where's this command?
　　　Poore man, thou searchest round
To finde out *death*, but missest *life* at hand.

Lent

Welcome deare feast of Lent: who loves not thee,
He loves not Temperance, or Authoritie,
　　　But is compos'd of passion.
The Scriptures bid us *fast*; the Church sayes, *now*:
Give to thy Mother, what thou wouldst allow
　　　To ev'ry Corporation.

The humble soul compos'd of love and fear
Begins at home, and layes the burden there,
　　　When doctrines disagree.
He sayes, in things which use hath justly got,
I am a scandall to the Church, and not
　　　The Church is so to me.

True Christians should be glad of an occasion
To use their temperance, seeking no evasion,
　　　When good is seasonable;
Unlesse Authoritie, which should increase
The obligation in us, make it lesse,
　　　And Power it self disable.

Besides the cleannesse of sweet abstinence,
Quick thoughts and motions at a small expense,
　　　A face not fearing light:
Whereas in fulnesse there are sluttish fumes,
Sowre exhalations, and dishonest rheumes,
　　　Revenging the delight.

Then those same pendant profits, which the spring
And Easter intimate, enlarge the thing,
   And goodnesse of the deed.
Neither ought other mens abuse of Lent
Spoil the good use; lest by that argument
   We forfeit all our Creed.

It's true, we cannot reach Christs forti'th day;
Yet to go part of that religious way,
   Is better then to rest:
We cannot reach our Saviours puritie;
Yet are we bid, *Be holy ev'n as he.*
   In both let's do our best.

Who goeth in the way which Christ hath gone,
Is much more sure to meet with him, then one
   That travelleth by-wayes:
Perhaps my God, though he be farre before,
May turn, and take me by the hand, and more
   May strengthen my decayes.

Yet Lord instruct us to improve our fast
By starving sinne and taking such repast
   As may our faults controll:
That ev'ry man may revell at his doore,
Not in his parlour; banquetting the poore,
   And among those his soul.

Vertue

SWEET day, so cool, so calm, so bright,
The bridall of the earth and skie:
The dew shall weep thy fall to night;
   For thou must die.

Sweet rose, whose hue angrie and brave
Bids the rash gazer wipe his eye:
Thy root is ever in its grave,
                              And thou must die.

Sweet spring, full of sweet dayes and roses,
A box where sweets compacted lie;
My musick shows ye have your closes,
                              And all must die.

Onely a sweet and vertuous soul,
Like season'd timber, never gives;
But though the whole world turn to coal,
                              Then chiefly lives.

The Pearl. Matt. 13. 45

I KNOW the wayes of Learning; both the head
And pipes that feed the presse, and make it runne;
What reason hath from nature borrowed,
Or of it self, like a good huswife, spunne
In laws and policie; what the starres conspire,
What willing nature speaks, what forc'd by fire;
Both th' old discoveries, and the new found seas,
The stock and surplus, cause and historie:
All these stand open, or I have the keyes:
                              Yet I love thee.

I know the wayes of Honour, what maintains
The quick returns of courtesie and wit:
In vies of favours whether partie gains,
When glorie swells the heart, and moldeth it
To all expressions both of hand and eye,
Which on the world a true love knot may tie,

And bear the bundle, wheresoe're it goes:
How many drammes of spirit there must be
To sell my life unto my friends or foes:
        Yet I love thee.

I know the wayes of Pleasure, the sweet strains,
The lullings and the relishes of it;
The propositions of hot bloud and brains;
What mirth and musick mean; what love and wit
Have done these twentie hundred yeares, and more:
I know the projects of unbridled store:
My stuffe is flesh, not brasse; my senses live,
And grumble oft, that they have more in me
Then he that curbs them, being but one to five:
        Yet I love thee.

I know all these, and have them in my hand:
Therefore not sealed, but with open eyes
I flie to thee, and fully understand
Both the main sale, and the commodities;
And at what rate and price I have thy love;
With all the circumstances that may move:
Yet through these labyrinths, not my groveling wit,
But thy silk twist let down from heav'n to me,
Did both conduct and teach me, how by it
        To climbe to thee.

Affliction (IV)

BROKEN in pieces all asunder,
        Lord, hunt me not,
        A thing forgot,
Once a poore creature, now a wonder,
        A wonder tortur'd in the space
        Betwixt this world and that of grace.

My thoughts are all a case of knives,
      Wounding my heart
      With scatter'd smart,
As watring pots give flowers their lives.
      Nothing their furie can controll,
      While they do wound and pink my soul.

All my attendants are at strife,
      Quitting their place
      Unto my face:
Nothing performs the task of life:
      The elements are let loose to fight,
      And while I live, trie out their right.

Oh help, my God! let not their plot
      Kill them and me,
      And also thee,
Who art my life: dissolve the knot,
      As the sunne scatters by his light
      All the rebellions of the night.

Then shall those powers, which work for grief,
      Enter thy pay,
      And day by day
Labour thy praise, and my relief;
      With care and courage building me,
      Till I reach heav'n, and much more, thee.

Man

      My God, I heard this day,
That none doth build a stately habitation,
      But he that means to dwell therein.
      What house more stately hath there been,
Or can be, then is Man? to whose creation
      All things are in decay.

For Man is ev'ry thing,
And more: He is a tree, yet bears more fruit;
A beast, yet is, or should be more:
Reason and speech we onely bring.
Parrats may thank us, if they are not mute,
They go upon the score.

Man is all symmetrie,
Full of proportions, one limbe to another,
And all to all the world besides:
Each part may call the furthest, brother:
For head with foot hath private amitie,
And both with moons and tides.

Nothing hath got so farre,
But man hath caught and kept it, as his prey.
His eyes dismount the highest starre:
He is in little all the sphere.
Herbs gladly cure our flesh; because that they
Finde their acquaintance there.

For us the windes do blow,
The earth doth rest, heav'n move, and fountains flow.
Nothing we see, but means our good,
As our delight, or as our treasure:
The whole is, either our cupboard of food,
Or cabinet of pleasure.

The starres have us to bed;
Night draws the curtain, which the sunne withdraws;
Musick and light attend our head.
All things unto our flesh are kinde
In their descent and being; to our minde
In their ascent and cause.

Each thing is full of dutie:
Waters united are our navigation;

Distinguished, our habitation;
Below, our drink; above, our meat;
Both are our cleanlinesse. Hath one such beautie?
    Then how are all things neat?

More servants wait on Man,
Then he'l take notice of: in ev'ry path
    He treads down that which doth befriend him,
When sicknesse makes him pale and wan.
Oh mightie love! Man is one world, and hath
    Another to attend him.

Since then, my God, thou hast
So brave a Palace built; O dwell in it,
    That it may dwell with thee at last!
Till then, afford us so much wit;
That, as the world serves us, we may serve thee,
    And both thy servants be.

Antiphon (II)

Chor. PRAISED be the God of love,
        Men.   Here below,
        Angels. And here above:
Cho. Who hath dealt his mercies so,
        Ang. To his friend,
        Men. And to his foe;

Cho. That both grace and glorie tend
        Ang. Us of old,
        Men. And us in th'end.
Cho. The great shepherd of the fold
        Ang. Us did make,
        Men. For us was sold.

Cho.   He our foes in pieces brake;
      Ang.   Him we touch;
      Men.   And him we take.

Cho.   Wherefore since that he is such,
      Ang.   We adore,
      Men.   And we do crouch.

Cho.   Lord, thy praises should be more.
      Men.   We have none,
      Ang.   And we no store.

Cho.   Praised be the God alone,
      Who hath made of two folds one.

Unkindnesse

LORD, make me coy and tender to offend:
In friendship, first I think, if that agree,
      Which I intend,
   Unto my friends intent and end.
I would not use a friend, as I use Thee.

If any touch my friend, or his good name,
It is my honour and my love to free
      His blasted fame
   From the least spot or thought of blame.
I could not use a friend, as I use Thee.

My friend may spit upon my curious floore:
Would he have gold? I lend it instantly;
      But let the poore,
   And thou within them, starve at doore.
I cannot use a friend, as I use Thee.

When that my friend pretendeth to a place,
I quit my interest, and leave it free:
      But when thy grace
   Sues for my heart, I thee displace,
Nor would I use a friend, as I use Thee.

Yet can a friend what thou hast done fulfill?
O write in brasse, *My God upon a tree*
> *His bloud did spill*
> *Onely to purchase my good-will.*
Yet use I not my foes, as I use Thee.

Life

I MADE a posie, while the day ran by:
Here will I smell my remnant out, and tie
> My life within this band.
But Time did becken to the flowers, and they
By noon most cunningly did steal away,
> And wither'd in my hand.

My hand was next to them, and then my heart:
I took, without more thinking, in good part
> Times gentle admonition:
Who did so sweetly deaths sad taste convey,
Making my minde to smell my fatall day;
> Yet sugring the suspicion.

Farewell deare flowers, sweetly your time ye spent,
Fit, while ye liv'd, for smell or ornament,
> And after death for cures.
I follow straight without complaints or grief,
Since if my sent be good, I care not if
> It be as short as yours.

Submission

BUT that thou art my wisdome, Lord.
> And both mine eyes are thine,
My minde would be extreamly stirr'd
> For missing my designe.

Were it not better to bestow
    Some place and power on me?
Then should thy praises with me grow,
    And share in my degree.

But when I thus dispute and grieve,
    I do resume my sight,
And pilfring what I once did give,
    Disseize thee of thy right.

How know I, if thou shouldst me raise,
    That I should then raise thee?
Perhaps great places and thy praise
    Do not so well agree.

Wherefore unto my gift I stand;
    I will no more advise:
Onely do thou lend me a hand,
    Since thou hast both mine eyes.

Justice (1)

I CANNOT skill of these thy wayes.
    Lord, thou didst make me, yet thou woundest me;
Lord, thou dost wound me, yet thou dost relieve me:
Lord, thou relievest, yet I die by thee:
Lord, thou dost kill me, yet thou dost reprieve me.

    But when I mark my life and praise,
    Thy justice me most fitly payes:
For, *I do praise thee, yet I praise thee not:*
My prayers mean thee, yet my prayers stray:
I would do well, yet sinne the hand hath got:
My soul doth love thee, yet it loves delay.
    I cannot skill of these my wayes.

Charms and Knots

Who reade a chapter when they rise,
Shall ne're be troubled with ill eyes.

A poore mans rod, when thou dost ride,
Is both a weapon and a guide.

Who shuts his hand, hath lost his gold:
Who opens it, hath it twice told.

Who goes to bed and does not pray,
Maketh two nights to ev'ry day.

Who by aspersions throw a stone
At th' head of others, hit their own.

Who looks on ground with humble eyes,
Findes himself there, and seeks to rise.

When th' hair is sweet through pride or lust,
The powder doth forget the dust.

Take one from ten, and what remains?
Ten still, if sermons go for gains.

In shallow waters heav'n doth show;
But who drinks on, to hell may go.

Affliction (v)

My God, I read this day,
That planted Paradise was not so firm,
As was and is thy floting Ark; whose stay
And anchor thou art onely, to confirm
        And strengthen it in ev'ry age,
        When waves do rise, and tempests rage.

At first we liv'd in pleasure;
Thine own delights thou didst to us impart:
When we grew wanton, thou didst use displeasure
To make us thine: yet that we might not part,
  As we at first did board with thee,
  Now thou wouldst taste our miserie.

  There is but joy and grief;
If either will convert us, we are thine:
Some Angels us'd the first; if our relief
Take up the second, then thy double line
  And sev'rall baits in either kinde
  Furnish thy table to thy minde.

  Affliction then is ours;
We are the trees, whom shaking fastens more,
While blustring windes destroy the wanton bowres
And ruffle all their curious knots and store.
  My God, so temper joy and wo,
  That thy bright beams may tame thy bow.

Mortification

  HOW soon doth man decay!
When clothes are taken from a chest of sweets
  To swaddle infants, whose young breath
  Scarce knows the way;
Those clouts are little winding sheets,
Which do consigne and send them unto death.

  When boyes go first to bed,
They step into their voluntarie graves,
  Sleep bindes them fast; onely their breath
  Makes them not dead:
Successive nights, like rolling waves,
Convey them quickly, who are bound for death.

When youth is frank and free,
And calls for musick, while his veins do swell,
    All day exchanging mirth and breath
        In companie;
    That musick summons to the knell,
Which shall befriend him at the houre of death.

When man grows staid and wise,
Getting a house and home, where he may move
    Within the circle of his breath,
        Schooling his eyes;
    That dumbe inclosure maketh love
Unto the coffin, that attends his death.

When age grows low and weak,
Marking his grave, and thawing ev'ry yeare,
    Till all do melt, and drown his breath
        When he would speak;
    A chair or litter shows the biere,
Which shall convey him to the house of death.

Man, ere he is aware,
Hath put together a solemnitie,
    And drest his herse, while he has breath
        As yet to spare:
    Yet Lord, instruct us so to die,
That all these dyings may be life in death.

Decay

SWEET were the dayes, when thou didst lodge with Lot,
Struggle with Jacob, sit with Gideon,
Advise with Abraham, when thy power could not
Encounter Moses strong complaints and mone:
    Thy words were then, *Let me alone.*

One might have sought and found thee presently
At some fair oak, or bush, or cave, or well:
Is my God this way? No, they would reply:
He is to Sinai gone, as we heard tell:
     List, ye may heare great Aarons bell.

But now thou dost thy self immure and close
In some one corner of a feeble heart:
Where yet both Sinne and Satan, thy old foes,
Do pinch and straiten thee, and use much art
     To gain thy thirds and little part.

I see the world grows old, when as the heat
Of thy great love, once spread, as in an urn
Doth closet up it self, and still retreat,
Cold Sinne still forcing it, till it return,
     And calling *Justice*, all things burn.

Miserie

    LORD, let the Angels praise thy name.
Man is a foolish thing, a foolish thing,
    Folly and Sinne play all his game.
His house still burns, and yet he still doth sing,
     Man is but grasse,
     He knows it, fill the glasse.

    How canst thou brook his foolishnesse?
Why, he'l not lose a cup of drink for thee:
    Bid him but temper his excesse;
Not he: he knows where he can better be,
     As he will swear,
     Then to serve thee in fear.

    What strange pollutions doth he wed,
And make his own? as if none knew but he.
    No man shall beat into his head,

That thou within his curtains drawn canst see:
        They are of cloth,
      Where never yet came moth.

  The best of men, turn but thy hand
For one poore minute, stumble at a pinne:
    They would not have their actions scann'd,
Nor any sorrow tell them that they sinne,
        Though it be small,
      And measure not their fall.

  They quarrell thee, and would give over
The bargain made to serve thee: but thy love
    Holds them unto it, and doth cover
Their follies with the wing of thy milde Dove,
        Not suff'ring those
      Who would, to be thy foes.

  My God, Man cannot praise thy name:
Thou art all brightnesse, perfect puritie;
    The sunne holds down his head for shame,
Dead with eclipses, when we speak of thee:
        How shall infection
      Presume on thy perfection?

  As dirtie hands foul all they touch,
And those things most, which are most pure and fine:
    So our clay hearts, ev'n when we crouch
To sing thy praises, make them lesse divine.
        Yet either this,
      Or none, thy portion is.

  Man cannot serve thee; let him go,
And serve the swine: there, there is his delight:
    He doth not like this vertue, no;
Give him his dirt to wallow in all night:
        These Preachers make
      His head to shoot and ake.

Oh foolish man! where are thine eyes?
How hast thou lost them in a croud of cares?
   Thou pull'st the rug, and wilt not rise,
No, not to purchase the whole pack of starres:
     There let them shine,
     Thou must go sleep, or dine.

The bird that sees a daintie bowre
Made in the tree, where she was wont to sit,
   Wonders and sings, but not his power
Who made the arbour: this exceeds her wit.
     But Man doth know
     The spring, whence all things flow:

And yet, as though he knew it not,
His knowledge winks, and lets his humours reigne;
   They make his life a constant blot,
And all the bloud of God to run in vain.
     Ah wretch! what verse
     Can thy strange wayes rehearse?

Indeed at first Man was a treasure,
A box of jewels, shop of rarities,
   A ring, whose posie was, *My pleasure:*
He was a garden in a Paradise:
     Glorie and grace
     Did crown his heart and face.

But sinne hath fool'd him. Now he is
A lump of flesh, without a foot or wing
   To raise him to a glimpse of blisse:
A sick toss'd vessel, dashing on each thing;
     Nay, his own shelf:
     My God, I mean my self.

Jordan (II)

WHEN first my lines of heav'nly joyes made mention,
Such was their lustre, they did so excell,
That I sought out quaint words, and trim invention;
My thoughts began to burnish, sprout, and swell,
Curling with metaphors a plain intention,
Decking the sense, as if it were to sell.

Thousands of notions in my brain did runne,
Off'ring their service, if I were not sped:
I often blotted what I had begunne;
This was not quick enough, and that was dead.
Nothing could seem too rich to clothe the sunne,
Much lesse those joyes which trample on his head.

As flames do work and winde, when they ascend,
So did I weave my self into the sense.
But while I bustled, I might heare a friend
Whisper, *How wide is all this long pretence!*
There is in love a sweetnesse readie penn'd:
Copie out onely that, and save expense.

Prayer (II)

OF what an easie quick accesse,
My blessed Lord, art thou! how suddenly
May our requests thine eare invade!
To shew that state dislikes not easinesse,
If I but lift mine eyes, my suit is made:
Thou canst no more not heare, then thou canst die.

Of what supreme almightie power
Is thy great arm, which spans the east and west,
And tacks the centre to the sphere!

By it do all things live their measur'd houre:
We cannot ask the thing, which is not there,
Blaming the shallownesse of our request.

Of what unmeasurable love
Art thou possest, who, when thou couldst not die,
    Wert fain to take our flesh and curse,
And for our sakes in person sinne reprove,
That by destroying that which ty'd thy purse,
Thou mightst make way for liberalitie!

Since then these three wait on thy throne,
Ease, Power, and *Love*; I value prayer so,
    That were I to leave all but one,
Wealth, fame, endowments, vertues, all should go;
I and deare prayer would together dwell,
And quickly gain, for each inch lost, an ell.

Obedience

My God, if writings may
Convey a Lordship any way
Whither the buyer and the seller please;
    Let it not thee displease,
If this poore paper do as much as they.

On it my heart doth bleed
As many lines, as there doth need
To passe it self and all it hath to thee.
    To which I do agree,
And here present it as my speciall Deed.

If that hereafter Pleasure
Cavill, and claim her part and measure,
As if this passed with a reservation,
    Or some such words in fashion;
I here exclude the wrangler from thy treasure.

O let thy sacred will
All thy delight in me fulfill!
Let me not think an action mine own way,
But as thy love shall sway,
Resigning up the rudder to thy skill.

Lord, what is man to thee,
That thou shouldst minde a rotten tree?
Yet since thou canst not choose but see my actions;
So great are thy perfections,
Thou mayst as well my actions guide, as see.

Besides, thy death and bloud
Show'd a strange love to all our good:
Thy sorrows were in earnest; no faint proffer,
Or superficiall offer
Of what we might not take, or be withstood.

Wherefore I all forgo:
To one word onely I say, No:
Where in the Deed there was an intimation
Of a gift or donation,
Lord, let it now by way of purchase go.

He that will passe his land,
As I have mine, may set his hand
And heart unto this Deed, when he hath read;
And make the purchase spread
To both our goods, if he to it will stand.

How happie were my part,
If some kinde man would thrust his heart
Into these lines; till in heav'ns Court of Rolls
They were by winged souls
Entred for both, farre above their desert!

Conscience

PEACE pratler, do not lowre:
Not a fair look, but thou dost call it foul:
Not a sweet dish, but thou dost call it sowre:
    Musick to thee doth howl.
  By listning to thy chatting fears
  I have both lost mine eyes and eares.

    Pratler, no more, I say:
My thoughts must work, but like a noiseless sphere;
Harmonious peace must rock them all the day:
    No room for pratlers there.
  If thou persistest, I will tell thee,
  That I have physick to expell thee.

    And the receit shall be
My Saviours bloud: when ever at his board
I do but taste it, straight it cleanseth me,
    And leaves thee not a word;
  No, not a tooth or nail to scratch,
  And at my actions carp, or catch.

    Yet if thou talkest still,
Besides my physick, know there's some for thee:
Some wood and nails to make a staffe or bill
    For those that trouble me:
  The bloudie crosse of my deare Lord
  Is both my physick and my sword.

Sion

LORD, with what glorie wast thou serv'd of old,
When Solomons temple stood and flourished!
    Where most things were of purest gold;
    The wood was all embellished
With flowers and carvings, mysticall and rare:
All show'd the builders, crav'd the seeers* care.

    * seers.

Yet all this glorie, all this pomp and state
Did not affect thee much, was not thy aim;
 Something there was, that sow'd debate:
 Wherefore thou quitt'st thy ancient claim:
And now thy Architecture meets with sinne;
For all thy frame and fabrick is within.

There thou art struggling with a peevish heart,
Which sometimes crosseth thee, thou sometimes it:
 The fight is hard on either part.
 Great God doth fight, he doth submit.
All Solomons sea of brasse and world of stone
Is not so deare to thee as one good grone.

And truly brasse and stones are heavie things,
Tombes for the dead, not temples fit for thee:
 But grones are quick, and full of wings,
 And all their motions upward be;
And ever·as they mount, like larks they sing;
The note is sad, yet musick for a King.

Home

COME Lord, my head doth burn, my heart is sick,
 While thou dost ever, ever stay:
Thy long deferrings wound me to the quick,
 My spirit gaspeth night and day.
  O show thy self to me,
  Or take me up to thee!

How canst thou stay, considering the pace
 The bloud did make, which thou didst waste?
When I behold it trickling down thy face,
 I never saw thing make such haste.
  O show thy, &c.

97

When man was lost, thy pitie lookt about
    To see what help in th' earth or skie:
But there was none; at least no help without:
    The help did in thy bosome lie.
        O show thy self to me,
        Or take me up to thee!

There lay thy sonne: and must he leave that nest,
    That hive of sweetnesse, to remove
Thraldome from those, who would not at a feast
    Leave one poore apple for thy love?
        O show thy, &c.

He did, he came: O my Redeemer deare,
    After all this canst thou be strange?
So many yeares baptiz'd, and not appeare?
    As if thy love could fail or change.
        O show thy, &c.

Yet if thou stayest still, why must I stay?
    My God, what is this world to me,
This world of wo? hence all ye clouds, away,
    Away; I must get up and see.
        O show thy, &c.

What is this weary world; this meat and drink,
    That chains us by the teeth so fast?
What is this woman-kinde, which I can wink
    Into a blacknesse and distaste?
        O show thy, &c.

With one small sigh thou gav'st me th' other day
    I blasted all the joyes about me:
And scouling on them as they pin'd away,
    Now come again, said I, and flout me.
        O show thy, &c.

Nothing but drought and dearth, but bush and brake,
　　Which way so-e're I look, I see.
Some may dream merrily, but when they wake,
　　They dresse themselves and come to thee.
　　　　O show thy self to me,
　　　　Or take me up to thee!

We talk of harvests; there are no such things,
　　But when we leave our corn and hay:
There is no fruitfull yeare, but that which brings
　　The last and lov'd, though dreadfull day.
　　　　O show thy, &c.

Oh loose this frame, this knot of man untie!
　　That my free soul may use her wing,
Which now is pinion'd with mortalitie,
　　As an intangled, hamper'd thing.
　　　　O show thy, &c.

What have I left, that I should stay and grone?
　　The most of me to heav'n is fled:
My thoughts and joyes are all packt up and gone,
　　And for their old acquaintance plead.
　　　　O show thy, &c.

Come dearest Lord, passe not this holy season,
　　My flesh and bones and joynts do pray:
And ev'n my verse, when by the ryme and reason
　　The word is, *Stay*, sayes ever, *Come*.
　　　　O show thy, &c.

The British Church

　　I JOY, deare Mother, when I view
　　Thy perfect lineaments and hue
　　　　　　　　Both sweet and bright.
　　Beautie in thee takes up her place,
　　And dates her letters from thy face,
　　　　　　　　When she doth write.

99

A fine aspect in fit aray,
Neither too mean, nor yet too gay,
          Shows who is best.
Outlandish looks may not compare:
For all they either painted are,
          Or else undrest.

She on the hills, which wantonly
Allureth all in hope to be
          By her preferr'd,
Hath kiss'd so long her painted shrines,
That ev'n her face by kissing shines,
          For her reward.

She in the valley is so shie
Of dressing, that her hair doth lie
          About her eares:
While she avoids her neighbours pride,
She wholly goes on th' other side,
          And nothing wears.

But, dearest Mother, what those misse,
The mean, thy praise and glorie is,
          And long may be.
Blessed be God, whose love it was
To double-moat thee with his grace,
          And none but thee.

The Quip

THE merrie world did on a day
  With his train-bands and mates agree
To meet together, where I lay,
  And all in sport to geere at me.

First, Beautie crept into a rose,
Which when I pluckt not, Sir, said she,
Tell me, I pray, Whose hands are those?
But thou shalt answer, Lord, for me.

Then Money came, and chinking still,
What tune is this, poore man? said he:
I heard in Musick you had skill.
But thou shalt answer, Lord, for me.

Then came brave Glorie puffing by
In silks that whistled, who but he?
He scarce allow'd me half an eie.
But thou shalt answer, Lord, for me.

Then came quick Wit and Conversation,
And he would needs a comfort be,
And, to be short, make an Oration.
But thou shalt answer, Lord, for me.

Yet when the houre of thy designe
To answer these fine things shall come;
Speak not at large; say, I am thine:
And then they have their answer home.

Vanitie (II)

POORE silly soul, whose hope and head lies low;
Whose flat delights on earth do creep and grow;
To whom the starres shine not so fair, as eyes;
Nor solid work, as false embroyderies;
Heark and beware, lest what you now do measure
And write for sweet, prove a most sowre displeasure.

O heare betimes, lest thy relenting
          May come too late!
To purchase heaven for repenting
          Is no hard rate.

If souls be made of earthly mold,
       Let them love gold;
       If born on high,
Let them unto their kindred flie:
   For they can never be at rest,
   Till they regain their ancient nest.
Then silly soul take heed; for earthly joy
Is but a bubble, and makes thee a boy.

The Dawning

AWAKE sad heart, whom sorrow ever drowns;
   Take up thine eyes, which feed on earth;
Unfold thy forehead gather'd into frowns:
   Thy Saviour comes, and with him mirth:
              Awake, awake;
And with a thankfull heart his comforts take.
   But thou dost still lament, and pine, and crie;
   And feel his death, but not his victorie.

Arise sad heart; if thou doe not withstand,
   Christs resurrection thine may be:
Do not by hanging down break from the hand,
   Which as it riseth, raiseth thee:
             Arise, arise;
And with his buriall-linen drie thine eyes:
   Christ left his grave-clothes, that we might, when grie
   Draws tears, or bloud, not want a handkerchief.

JESU

JESU is in my heart, his sacred name
Is deeply carved there: but th' other week
A great affliction broke the little frame,
Ev'n all to pieces: which I went to seek:

And first I found the corner, where was *J*,
After, where *ES*, and next where *U* was graved.
When I had got these parcels, instantly
I sat me down to spell them, and perceived
That to my broken heart he was *I ease you*,
   And to my whole is *JESU*.

Businesse

  CANST be idle? canst thou play,
  Foolish soul who sinn'd to day?

Rivers run, and springs each one
Know their home, and get them gone:
Hast thou tears, or hast thou none?

If, poore soul, thou hast no tears,
Would thou hadst no faults or fears!
Who hath these, those ill forbears.

Windes still work: it is their plot,
Be the season cold, or hot:
Hast thou sighs, or hast thou not?

If thou hast no sighs or grones,
Would thou hadst no flesh and bones!
Lesser pains scape greater ones.

  But if yet thou idle be,
  Foolish soul, Who di'd for thee?

Who did leave his Fathers throne,
To assume thy flesh and bone;
Had he life, or had he none?

If he had not liv'd for thee,
Thou hadst di'd most wretchedly;
And two deaths had been thy fee.

He so farre thy good did plot,
That his own self he forgot.
Did he die, or did he not?

If he had not di'd for thee,
Thou hadst liv'd in miserie.
Two lives worse then ten deaths be.

    And hath any space of breath
      'Twixt his sinnes and Saviours death?

He that loseth gold, though drosse,
Tells to all he meets, his crosse:
He that sinnes, hath he no losse?

He that findes a silver vein,
Thinks on it, and thinks again:
Brings thy Saviours death no gain?

    Who in heart not ever kneels,
      Neither sinne nor Saviour feels.

Dialogue

SWEETEST Saviour, if my soul
    Were but worth the having,
Quickly should I then controll
    Any thought of waving.
But when all my care and pains
Cannot give the name of gains
To thy wretch so full of stains,
What delight or hope remains?

What, Child, is the ballance thine,
    Thine the poise and measure?
If I say, Thou shalt be mine;
    Finger not my treasure.

What the gains in having thee
Do amount to, onely he,
Who for man was sold, can see;
That transferr'd th' accounts to me.

But as I can see no merit,
        Leading to this favour:
So the way to fit me for it
        Is beyond my savour.
As the reason then is thine;
So the way is none of mine:
I disclaim the whole designe:
Sinne disclaims and I resigne.

That is all, if that I could
        Get without repining;
And my clay, my creature, would
        Follow my resigning:
That as I did freely part
With my glorie and desert,
Left all joyes to feel all smart——
        Ah! no more: thou break'st my heart.

Dulnesse

WHY do I languish thus, drooping and dull,
        As if I were all earth?
O give me quicknesse, that I may with mirth
        Praise thee brim-full!

The wanton lover in a curious strain
        Can praise his fairest fair;
And with quaint metaphors her curled hair
        Curl o're again.

Thou art my lovelinesse, my life, my light,
         Beautie alone to me:
Thy bloudy death and undeserv'd, makes thee
           Pure red and white.

When all perfections as but one appeare,
         That those thy form doth show,
The very dust, where thou dost tread and go,
          Makes beauties here.

Where are my lines then? my approaches? views?
         Where are my window-songs?
Lovers are still pretending, & ev'n wrongs
          Sharpen their Muse:

But I am lost in flesh, whose sugred lyes
         Still mock me, and grow bold:
Sure thou didst put a minde there, if I could
          Finde where it lies.

Lord, cleare thy gift, that with a constant wit
         I may but look towards thee:
Look onely; for to *love* thee, who can be,
          What angel fit?

Love-joy

As on a window late I cast mine eye,
I saw a vine drop grapes with *J* and *C*
Anneal'd on every bunch. One standing by
Ask'd what it meant. I, who am never loth
To spend my judgement, said, It seem'd to me
To be the bodie and the letters both
Of *Joy* and *Charitie*. Sir, you have not miss'd,
The man reply'd; It figures *JESUS CHRIST*.

Providence

O SACRED Providence, who from end to end
Strongly and sweetly movest, shall I write,
And not of thee, through whom my fingers bend
To hold my quill? shall they not do thee right?

Of all the creatures both in sea and land
Onely to Man thou hast made known thy wayes.
And put the penne alone into his hand,
And made him Secretarie of thy praise.

Beasts fain would sing; birds dittie to their notes;
Trees would be tuning on their native lute
To thy renown: but all their hands and throats
Are brought to Man, while they are lame and mute.

Man is the worlds high Priest: he doth present
The sacrifice for all; while they below
Unto the service mutter an assent,
Such as springs use that fall, and windes that blow.

He that to praise and laud thee doth refrain,
Doth not refrain unto himself alone,
But robs a thousand who would praise thee fain,
And doth commit a world of sinne in one.

The beasts say, Eat me: but, if beasts must teach,
The tongue is yours to eat, but mine to praise.
The trees say, Pull me: but the hand you stretch,
Is mine to write, as it is yours to raise.

Wherefore, most sacred Spirit, I here present
For me and all my fellows praise to thee:
And just it is that I should pay the rent,
Because the benefit accrues to me.

We all acknowledge both thy power and love
To be exact, transcendent, and divine;
Who dost so strongly and so sweetly move,
While all things have their will, yet none but thine.

For either thy command or thy permission
Lay hands on all: they are thy right and left.
The first puts on with speed and expedition;
The other curbs sinnes stealing pace and theft.

Nothing escapes them both; all must appeare,
And be dispos'd, and dress'd, and tun'd by thee,
Who sweetly temper'st all. If we could heare
Thy skill and art, what musick would it be!

Thou art in small things great, not small in any:
Thy even praise can neither rise, nor fall.
Thou art in all things one, in each thing many:
For thou art infinite in one and all.

Tempests are calm to thee; they know thy hand,
And hold it fast, as children do their fathers,
Which crie and follow. Thou hast made poore sand
Check the proud sea, ev'n when it swells and gathers.

Thy cupboard serves the world: the meat is set,
Where all may reach: no beast but knows his feed.
Birds teach us hawking; fishes have their net:
The great prey on the lesse, they on some weed.

Nothing ingendred doth prevent his meat:
Flies have their table spread, ere they appeare.
Some creatures have in winter what to eat;
Others do sleep, and envie not their cheer.

How finely dost thou times and seasons spin,
And make a twist checker'd with night and day!
Which as it lengthens windes, and windes us in,
As bouls go on, but turning all the way.

Each creature hath a wisdome for his good.
The pigeons feed their tender off-spring, crying,
When they are callow; but withdraw their food
When they are fledge, that need may teach them flying.

Bees work for man; and yet they never bruise
Their masters flower, but leave it, having done,
As fair as ever, and as fit to use;
So both the flower doth stay, and hony run.

Sheep eat the grasse, and dung the ground for more:
Trees after bearing drop their leaves for soil:
Springs vent their streams, and by expense get store:
Clouds cool by heat, and baths by cooling boil.

Who hath the vertue to expresse the rare
And curious vertues both of herbs and stones?
Is there an herb for that? O that thy care
Would show a root, that gives expressions!

And if a herb hath power, what have the starres?
A rose, besides his beautie, is a cure.
Doubtlesse our plagues and plentie, peace and warres
Are there much surer then our art is sure.

Thou hast hid metals: man may take them thence;
But at his perill: when he digs the place,
He makes a grave; as if the thing had sense,
And threatned man, that he should fill the space.

Ev'n poysons praise thee. Should a thing be lost?
Should creatures want for want of heed their due?
Since where are poysons, antidotes are most:
The help stands close, and keeps the fear in view.

The sea, which seems to stop the traveller,
Is by a ship the speedier passage made.

The windes, who think they rule the mariner,
Are rul'd by him, and taught to serve his trade.

And as thy house is full, so I adore
Thy curious art in marshalling thy goods.
The hills with health abound; the vales with store;
The South with marble; North with furres & woods.

Hard things are glorious; easie things good cheap.
The common all men have; that which is rare
Men therefore seek to have, and care to keep.
The healthy frosts with summer-fruits compare.

Light without winde is glasse: warm without weight
Is wooll and furre: cool without closenesse, shade:
Speed without pains, a horse: tall without height,
A servile hawk: low without losse, a spade.

All countreys have enough to serve their need:
If they seek fine things, thou dost make them run
For their offence; and then dost turn their speed
To be commerce and trade from sunne to sunne.

Nothing wears clothes, but Man; nothing doth need
But he to wear them. Nothing useth fire,
But Man alone, to show his heav'nly breed:
And onely he hath fuell in desire.

When th' earth was dry, thou mad'st a sea of wet:
When that lay gather'd, thou didst broach the mountains
When yet some places could no moisture get,
The windes grew gard'ners, and the clouds good fountains

Rain, do not hurt my flowers; but gently spend
Your hony drops: presse not to smell them here:
When they are ripe, their odour will ascend,
And at your lodging with their thanks appeare.

How harsh are thorns to pears! and yet they make
A better hedge, and need lesse reparation.
How smooth are silks compared with a stake,
Or with a stone! yet make no good foundation.

Sometimes thou dost divide thy gifts to man,
Sometimes unite. The Indian nut alone
Is clothing, meat and trencher, drink and can,
Boat, cable, sail and needle, all in one.

Most herbs that grow in brooks, are hot and dry.
Cold fruits warm kernells help against the winde.
The lemmons juice and rinde cure mutually.
The whey of milk doth loose, the milk doth binde.

Thy creatures leap not, but expresse a feast,
Where all the guests sit close, and nothing wants.
Frogs marry fish and flesh; bats, bird and beast;
Sponges, non-sense and sense; mines, th' earth & plants.

To show thou art not bound, as if thy lot
Were worse then ours, sometimes thou shiftest hands.
Most things move th' under-jaw; the Crocodile not.
Most things sleep lying; th' Elephant leans or stands.

But who hath praise enough? nay, who hath any?
None can expresse thy works, but he that knows them:
And none can know thy works, which are so many,
And so complete, but onely he that owes them.

All things that are, though they have sev'rall wayes,
Yet in their being joyn with one advise
To honour thee: and so I give thee praise
In all my other hymnes, but in this twice.

Each thing that is, although in use and name
It go for one, hath many wayes in store
To honour thee; and so each hymne thy fame
Extolleth many wayes, yet this one more.

Hope

I GAVE to Hope a watch of mine: but he
          An anchor gave to me.
Then an old prayer-book I did present:
          And he an optick sent.
With that I gave a viall full of tears:
          But he a few green eares.
Ah Loyterer! I'le no more, no more I'le bring:
          I did expect a ring.

Sinnes round

SORRIE I am, my God, sorrie I am,
That my offences course it in a ring.
My thoughts are working like a busie flame,
Untill their cockatrice they hatch and bring:
And when they once have perfected their draughts,
My words take fire from my inflamed thoughts.

My words take fire from my inflamed thoughts,
Which spit it forth like the Sicilian Hill.
They vent the wares, and passe them with their faults,
And by their breathing ventilate the ill.
But words suffice not, where are lewd intentions:
My hands do joyn to finish the inventions.

My hands do joyn to finish the inventions:
And so my sinnes ascend three stories high,
As Babel grew, before there were dissensions.
Yet ill deeds loyter not: for they supplie
New thoughts of sinning: wherefore, to my shame,
Sorrie I am, my God, sorrie I am.

Time

MEETING with Time, Slack thing, said I,
Thy sithe is dull; whet it for shame.
No marvell Sir, he did replie,
If it at length deserve some blame:
   But where one man would have me grinde it,
   Twentie for one too sharp do finde it.

Perhaps some such of old did passe,
Who above all things lov'd this life;
To whom thy sithe a hatchet was,
Which now is but a pruning-knife.
   Christs coming hath made man thy debter,
   Since by thy cutting he grows better.

And in his blessing thou art blest:
For where thou onely wert before
An executioner at best;
Thou art a gard'ner now, and more,
   An usher to convey our souls
   Beyond the utmost starres and poles.

And this is that makes life so long,
While it detains us from our God.
Ev'n pleasures here increase the wrong,
And length of dayes lengthen the rod.
   Who wants the place, where God doth dwell,
   Partakes already half of hell.

Of what strange length must that needs be,
Which ev'n eternitie excludes!
Thus farre Time heard me patiently:
Then chafing said, This man deludes:
   What do I here before his doore?
   He doth not crave lesse time, but more.

Gratefulnesse

THOU that hast giv'n so much to me,
Give one thing more, a gratefull heart.
See how thy beggar works on thee
       By art.

He makes thy gifts occasion more,
And sayes, If he in this be crost,
All thou hast giv'n him heretofore
       Is lost.

But thou didst reckon, when at first
Thy word our hearts and hands did crave,
What it would come to at the worst
       To save.

Perpetuall knockings at thy doore,
Tears sullying thy transparent rooms,
Gift upon gift, much would have more,
       And comes.

This notwithstanding, thou wentst on,
And didst allow us all our noise:
Nay, thou hast made a sigh and grone
       Thy joyes.

Not that thou hast not still above
Much better tunes, then grones can make;
But that these countrey-aires thy love
       Did take.

Wherefore I crie, and crie again;
And in no quiet canst thou be,
Till I a thankfull heart obtain
       Of thee:

Not thankfull, when it pleaseth me;
As if thy blessings had spare dayes:
But such a heart, whose pulse may be
$\qquad$ Thy praise.

Peace

SWEET Peace, where dost thou dwell? I humbly crave,
$\qquad$ Let me once know.
I sought thee in a secret cave,
$\qquad$ And ask'd, if Peace were there.
A hollow winde did seem to answer, No:
$\qquad$ Go seek elsewhere.

I did; and going did a rainbow note:
$\qquad$ Surely, thought I,
This is the lace of Peaces coat:
$\qquad$ I will search out the matter.
But while I lookt, the clouds immediately
$\qquad$ Did break and scatter.

Then went I to a garden, and did spy
$\qquad$ A gallant flower,
The Crown Imperiall: Sure, said I,
$\qquad$ Peace at the root must dwell.
But when I digg'd, I saw a worm devoure
$\qquad$ What show'd so well.

At length I met a rev'rend good old man,
$\qquad$ Whom when for Peace
I did demand, he thus began:
$\qquad$ There was a Prince of old
At Salem dwelt, who liv'd with good increase
$\qquad$ Of flock and fold.

He sweetly liv'd; yet sweetnesse did not save
              His life from foes.
  But after death out of his grave
      There sprang twelve stalks of wheat:
Which many wondring at, got some of those
              To plant and set.

It prosper'd strangely, and did soon disperse
              Through all the earth:
  For they that taste it do rehearse,
      That vertue lies therein,
A secret vertue bringing peace and mirth
              By flight of sinne.

Take of this grain, which in my garden grows,
              And grows for you;
  Make bread of it: and that repose
      And peace, which ev'ry where
With so much earnestnesse you do pursue,
              Is onely there.

Confession

    O WHAT a cunning guest
Is this same grief! within my heart I made
    Closets; and in them many a chest;
    And, like a master in my trade,
In those chests, boxes; in each box, a till:
Yet grief knows all, and enters when he will.

    No scrue, no piercer can
Into a piece of timber work and winde,
    As Gods afflictions into man,
    When he a torture hath design'd
They are too subtill for the subt'llest hearts;
And fall, like rheumes, upon the tendrest parts.

We are the earth; and they,
Like moles within us, heave, and cast about:
    And till they foot and clutch their prey,
        They never cool, much lesse give out.
No smith can make such locks but they have keyes:
Closets are halls to them; and hearts, high-wayes.

        Onely an open breast
Doth shut them out, so that they cannot enter;
    Or, if they enter, cannot rest,
        But quickly seek some new adventure.
Smooth open hearts no fastning have; but fiction
Doth give a hold and handle to affliction.

        Wherefore my faults and sinnes,
Lord, I acknowledge; take thy plagues away:
    For since confession pardon winnes,
        I challenge here the brightest day,
The clearest diamond: let them do their best,
They shall be thick and cloudie to my breast.

Giddinesse

OH, what a thing is man! how farre from power,
        From setled peace and rest!
He is some twentie sev'rall men at least
        Each sev'rall houre.

One while he counts of heav'n, as of his treasure:
        But then a thought creeps in,
And calls him coward, who for fear of sinne
        Will lose a pleasure.

Now he will fight it out, and to the warres;
        Now eat his bread in peace,
And snudge in quiet: now he scorns increase;
        Now all day spares.

117

He builds a house, which quickly down must go,
   As if a whirlwinde blew
And crusht the building: and it's partly true,
   His minde is so.

O what a sight were Man, if his attires
   Did alter with his minde;
And like a Dolphins skinne, his clothes combin'd
   With his desires!

Surely if each one saw anothers heart,
   There would be no commerce,
No sale or bargain passe: all would disperse,
   And live apart,

Lord, mend or rather make us: one creation
   Will not suffice our turn:
Except thou make us dayly, we shall spurn
   Our own salvation.

The Bunch of Grapes

JOY, I did lock thee up: but some bad man
   Hath let thee out again:
And now, me thinks, I am where I began
   Sev'n yeares ago: one vogue and vein,
   One aire of thoughts usurps my brain.
I did towards Canaan draw; but now I am
Brought back to the Red sea, the sea of shame.

For as the Jews of old by Gods command
   Travell'd, and saw no town;
So now each Christian hath his journeys spann'd:
   Their storie pennes and sets us down.
   A single deed is small renown.
Gods works are wide, and let in future times;
His ancient justice overflows our crimes.

Then we have too our guardian fires and clouds;
    Our Scripture dew drops fast:
We have our sands and serpents, tents and shrowds;
    Alas! our murmurings come not last.
     But where's the cluster? where's the taste
Of mine inheritance? Lord, if I must borrow,
Let me as well take up their joy, as sorrow.

But can he want the grape, who hath the wine?
    I have their fruit and more.
Blessed be God, who prosper'd *Noahs* vine,
    And made it bring forth grapes good store,
     But much more him I must adore,
Who of the Laws sowre juice sweet wine did make,
Ev'n God himself being pressed for my sake.

Love unknown

DEARE Friend, sit down, the tale is long and sad:
And in my faintings I presume your love
Will more complie then help. A Lord I had,
And have, of whom some grounds, which may improve,
I hold for two lives, and both lives in me.
To him I brought a dish of fruit one day,
And in the middle plac'd my heart. But he
        (I sigh to say)
Lookt on a servant, who did know his eye
Better then you know me, or (which is one)
Then I my self. The servant instantly
Quitting the fruit, seiz'd on my heart alone,
And threw it in a font, wherein did fall
A stream of bloud, which issu'd from the side
Of a great rock: I well remember all,
And have good cause: there it was dipt and dy'd,

And washt, and wrung: the very wringing yet
Enforceth tears. *Your heart was foul, I fear.*
Indeed 'tis true. I did and do commit
Many a fault more then my lease will bear;
Yet still askt pardon, and was not deni'd.
But you shall heare. After my heart was well,
And clean and fair, as I one eventide

(I sigh to tell)

Walkt by my self abroad, I saw a large
And spacious fornace flaming, and thereon
A boyling caldron, round about whose verge
Was in great letters set *AFFLICTION*.
The greatnesse shew'd the owner. So I went
To fetch a sacrifice out of my fold,
Thinking with that, which I did thus present,
To warm his love, which I did fear grew cold.
But as my heart did tender it, the man,
Who was to take it from me, slipt his hand,
And threw my heart into the scalding pan;
My heart, that brought it (do you understand?)
The offerers heart. *Your heart was hard, I fear.*
Indeed it's true. I found a callous matter
Began to spread and to expatiate there:
But with a richer drug then scalding water
I bath'd it often, ev'n with holy bloud,
Which at a board, while many drunk bare wine,
A friend did steal into my cup for good,
Ev'n taken inwardly, and most divine
To supple hardnesse. But at the length
Out of the caldron getting, soon I fled
Unto my house, where to repair the strength
Which I had lost, I hasted to my bed.
But when I thought to sleep out all these faults

(I sigh to speak

I found that some had stuff'd the bed with thoughts,
I would say *thorns*. Deare, could my heart not break,
When with my pleasures ev'n my rest was gone?
Full well I understood, who had been there:
For I had giv'n the key to none, but one:
It must be he. *Your heart was dull, I fear.*
Indeed a slack and sleepie state of minde
Did oft possesse me, so that when I pray'd,
Though my lips went, my heart did stay behinde.
But all my scores were by another paid.
Who took the debt upon him. *Truly, Friend,*
For ought I heare, your Master shows to you
More favour then you wot of. Mark the end.
The Font did onely, what was old, renew:
The Caldron suppled, what was grown too hard:
The Thorns did quicken, what was grown too dull:
All did but strive to mend, what you had marr'd.
Wherefore be cheer'd, and praise him to the full
Each day, each houre, each moment of the week,
Who fain would have you be new, tender, quick.

Mans medley

HEARK, how the birds do sing,
   And woods do ring.
All creatures have their joy: and man hath his.
   Yet if we rightly measure,
    Mans joy and pleasure
Rather hereafter, then in present, is.

   To this life things of sense
    Make their pretence:
In th' other Angels have a right by birth:
   Man ties them both alone,
    And makes them one,
With th' one hand touching heav'n, with th' other earth.

In soul he mounts and flies,
In flesh he dies.
He wears a stuffe whose thread is course and round,
But trimm'd with curious lace,
And should take place
After the trimming, not the stuffe and ground.

Not that he may not here
Taste of the cheer,
But as birds drink, and straight lift up their head,
So he must sip and think
Of better drink
He may attain to, after he is dead.

But as his joyes are double;
So is his trouble.
He hath two winters, other things but one:
Both frosts and thoughts do nip,
And bite his lip;
And he of all things fears two deaths alone.

Yet ev'n the greatest griefs
May be reliefs,
Could he but take them right, and in their wayes.
Happie is he, whose heart
Hath found the art
To turn his double pains to double praise.

The Storm

IF as the windes and waters here below
Do flie and flow,
My sighs and tears as busie were above;
Sure they would move
And much affect thee, as tempestuous times
Amaze poore mortals, and object their crimes.

Starres have their storms, ev'n in a high degree,
         As well as we.
A throbbing conscience spurred by remorse
         Hath a strange force:
It quits the earth, and mounting more and more
Dares to assault thee, and besiege thy doore.

There it stands knocking, to thy musicks wrong,
         And drowns the song.
Glorie and honour are set by, till it
         An answer get.
Poets have wrong'd poore storms: such dayes are best;
They purge the aire without, within the breast.

Paradise

I BLESSE thee, Lord, because I GROW
Among thy trees, which in a ROW
To thee both fruit and order OW.

What open force, or hidden CHARM
Can blast my fruit, or bring me HARM,
While the inclosure is thine ARM?

Inclose me still for fear I START.
Be to me rather sharp and TART,
Then let me want thy hand & ART.

When thou dost greater judgements SPARE,
And with thy knife but prune and PARE,
Ev'n fruitfull trees more fruitfull ARE.

Such sharpnes shows the sweetest FREND:
Such cuttings rather heal then REND:
And such beginnings touch their END.

The Method

POORE heart, lament.
For since thy God refuseth still,
There is some rub, some discontent,
            Which cools his will.

            Thy Father could
Quickly effect, what thou dost move;
For he is *Power*: and sure he would;
            For he is *Love*.

            Go search this thing,
Tumble thy breast, and turn thy book.
If thou hadst lost a glove or ring,
            Wouldst thou not look?

            What do I see
Written above there? *Yesterday*
I did behave me carelessly,
            When I did pray.

            And should Gods eare
To such indifferents chained be,
Who do not their own motions heare?
            Is God lesse free?

            But stay! what's there?
Late when I would have something done,
I had a motion to forbear,
            Yet I went on.

            And should Gods eare,
Which needs not man, be ty'd to those
Who heare not him, but quickly heare
            His utter foes?

>   Then once more pray:
> Down with thy knees, up with thy voice.
> Seek pardon first, and God will say,
>   *Glad heart rejoyce.*

Divinitie

As men, for fear the starres should sleep and nod,
    And trip at night, have spheres suppli'd;
As if a starre were duller then a clod,
    Which knows his way without a guide:

Just so the other heav'n they also serve,
    Divinities transcendent skie:
Which with the edge of wit they cut and carve.
    Reason triumphs, and faith lies by.

Could not that Wisdome, which first broacht the wine,
    Have thicken'd it with definitions?
And jagg'd his seamlesse coat, had that been fine,
    With curious questions and divisions?

But all the doctrine, which he taught and gave,
    Was cleare as heav'n, from whence it came.
At least those beams of truth, which onely save,
    Surpasse in brightnesse any flame.

Love God, and love your neighbour. Watch and pray.
    Do as ye would be done unto.
O dark instructions; ev'n as dark as day!
    Who can these Gordian knots undo?

But he doth bid us take his bloud for wine.
    Bid what he please; yet I am sure,
To take and taste what he doth there designe,
    Is all that saves, and not obscure.

Then burn thy Epicycles, foolish man;
    Break all thy spheres, and save thy head.
Faith needs no staffe of flesh, but stoutly can
    To heav'n alone both go, and leade

Ephes. 4. 30

Grieve not the Holy Spirit, &c.

AND art thou grieved, sweet and sacred Dove,
    When I am sowre,
    And crosse thy love?
Grieved for me? the God of strength and power
    Griev'd for a worm, which when I tread,
    I passe away and leave it dead?

Then weep mine eyes, the God of love doth grieve:
    Weep foolish heart,
    And weeping live:
For death is drie as dust. Yet if ye part,
    End as the night, whose sable hue
    Your sinnes expresse; melt into dew.

When sawcie mirth shall knock or call at doore,
    Cry out, Get hence,
    Or cry no more.
Almightie God doth grieve, he puts on sense:
    I sinne not to my grief alone,
    But to my Gods too; he doth grone.

Oh take thy lute, and tune it to a strain,
    Which may with thee
    All day complain.
There can no discord but in ceasing be.
    Marbles can weep; and surely strings
    More bowels have, then such hard things.

Lord, I adjudge my self to tears and grief,
      Ev'n endlesse tears
      Without relief.
If a cleare spring for me no time forbears,
      But runnes, although I be not drie;
      I am no Crystall, what shall I?

Yet if I wail not still, since still to wail
      Nature denies;
      And flesh would fail,
If my deserts were masters of mine eyes:
      Lord, pardon, for thy Sonne makes good
      My want of tears with store of bloud.

The Familie

WHAT doth this noise of thoughts within my heart,
      As if they had a part?
What do these loud complaints and puling fears,
      As if there were no rule or eares?

But, Lord, the house and familie are thine,
      Though some of them repine.
Turn out these wranglers, which defile thy seat:
      For where thou dwellest all is neat.

First Peace and Silence all disputes controll,
      Then Order plaies the soul;
And giving all things their set forms and houres,
      Makes of wilde woods sweet walks and bowres.

Humble Obedience neare the doore doth stand,
      Expecting a command:
Then whom in waiting nothing seems more slow,
      Nothing more quick when she doth go.

Joyes oft are there, and griefs as oft as joyes;
   But griefs without a noise:
Yet speak they louder then distemper'd fears.
  What is so shrill as silent tears?

This is thy house, with these it doth abound:
   And where these are not found,
Perhaps thou com'st sometimes, and for a day;
  But not to make a constant stay.

The Size

  CONTENT thee, greedie heart,
Modest and moderate joyes to those, that have
Title to more hereafter when they part,
   Are passing brave.
  Let th' upper springs into the low
  Descend and fall, and thou dost flow.

  What though some have a fraught
Of cloves and nutmegs, and in cinamon sail;
If thou hast wherewithall to spice a draught,
   When griefs prevail;
  And for the future time art heir
  To th' Isle of spices, is't not fair?

  To be in both worlds full
Is more then God was, who was hungrie here.
Wouldst thou his laws of fasting disanull?
   Enact good cheer?
  Lay out thy joy, yet hope to save it?
  Wouldst thou both eat thy cake, and have it?

  Great joyes are all at once;
But little do reserve themselves for more:

Those have their hopes; these what they have renounce,
        And live on score:
    Those are at home; these journey still,
    And meet the rest on Sions hill.

      Thy Saviour sentenc'd joy,
And in the flesh condemn'd it as unfit,
At least in lump: for such doth oft destroy;
          Whereas a bit
    Doth tice us on to hopes of more,
    And for the present health restore.

      A Christians state and case
Is not a corpulent, but a thinne and spare,
Yet active strength: whose long and bonie face
          Content and care
    Do seem to equally divide,
    Like a pretender, not a bride.

      Wherefore sit down, good heart;
Grasp not at much, for fear thou losest all.
If comforts fell according to desert,
    They would great frosts and snows destroy:
    For we should count, Since the last joy.

      Then close again the seam,
Which thou hast open'd: do not spread thy robe
In hope of great things. Call to minde thy dream,
          An earthly globe,
    On whose meridian was engraven,
    These seas are tears, and heav'n the haven.

Artillerie

As I one ev'ning sat before my cell,
Me thoughts a starre did shoot into my lap.
I rose, and shook my clothes, as knowing well,
That from small fires comes oft no small mishap.

When suddenly I heard one say,
Do as thou usest, disobey,
Expell good motions from thy breast,
Which have the face of fire, but end in rest.

I, who had heard of musick in the spheres,
But not of speech in starres, began to muse:
But turning to my God, whose ministers
The starres and all things are; If I refuse,
    Dread Lord, said I, so oft my good;
    Then I refuse not ev'n with bloud
    To wash away my stubborn thought:
For I will do or suffer what I ought.

But I have also starres and shooters too,
Born where thy servants both artilleries use.
My tears and prayers night and day do wooe,
And work up to thee; yet thou dost refuse.
    Not but I am (I must say still)
    Much more oblig'd to do thy will,
    Then thou to grant mine: but because
Thy promise now hath ev'n set thee thy laws.

Then we are shooters both, and thou dost deigne
To enter combate with us, and contest
With thine own clay. But I would parley fain:
Shunne not my arrows, and behold my breast.
    Yet if thou shunnest, I am thine:
    I must be so, if I am mine.
    There is no articling with thee:
I am but finite, yet thine infinitely.

Church-rents and schismes

BRAVE rose, (alas!) where art thou? in the chair
Where thou didst lately so triumph and shine

A worm doth sit, whose many feet and hair
Are the more foul, the more thou wert divine.
This, this hath done it, this did bite the root
And bottome of the leaves: which when the winde
Did once perceive, it blew them under foot,
Where rude unhallow'd steps do crush and grinde
    Their beauteous glories. Onely shreds of thee,
    And those all bitten, in thy chair I see.

Why doth my Mother blush? is she the rose,
And shows it so? Indeed Christs precious bloud
Gave you a colour once; which when your foes
Thought to let out, the bleeding did you good,
And made you look much fresher then before.
But when debates and fretting jealousies
Did worm and work within you more and more,
Your colour vaded,* and calamities
    Turned your ruddie into pale and bleak:
    Your health and beautie both began to break.

Then did your sev'rall parts unloose and start:
Which when your neighbours saw, like a north-winde
They rushed in, and cast them in the dirt
Where Pagans tread. O Mother deare and kinde,
Where shall I get me eyes enough to weep,
As many eyes as starres? since it is night,
And much of Asia and Europe fast asleep,
And ev'n all Africk; would at least I might
    With these two poore ones lick up all the dew,
    Which falls by night, and poure it out for you!

Justice (II)

O DREADFULL Justice, what a fright and terrour
        Wast thou of old,
           When sinne and errour

* faded.

Did show and shape thy looks to me,
   And through their glasse discolour thee
He that did but look up, was proud and bold.

The dishes of thy ballance seem'd to gape,
    Like two great pits;
    The beam and scape
  Did like some torturing engine show;
  Thy hand above did burn and glow,
Danting the stoutest hearts, the proudest wits.

But now that Christs pure vail presents the sight,
    I see no fears:
    Thy hand is white,
  Thy scales like buckets, which attend
  And interchangeably descend,
Lifting to heaven from this well of tears.

For where before thou still didst call on me,
    Now I still touch
    And harp on thee.
  Gods promises have made thee mine;
  Why should I justice now decline?
Against me there is none, but for me much.

The Pilgrimage

I TRAVELL'D on, seeing the hill, where lay
    My expectation.
  A long it was and weary way.
  The gloomy cave of Desperation
I left on th' one, and on the other side
    The rock of Pride.

And so I came to Fancies medow strow'd
    With many a flower:
  Fain would I here have made abode,
  But I was quicken'd by my houre.

So to Cares cops I came, and there got through
                    With much ado.

That led me to the wilde of Passion, which
                    Some call the wold;
        A wasted place, but sometimes rich.
            Here I was robb'd of all my gold,
Save one good Angell, which a friend had ti'd
                    Close to my side.

At length I got unto the gladsome hill,
                    Where lay my hope,
        Where lay my heart; and climbing still,
            When I had gain'd the brow and top,
A lake of brackish waters on the ground
                    Was all I found.

With that abash'd and struck with many a sting
                    Of swarming fears,
        I fell, and cry'd, Alas my King!
            Can both the way and end be tears?
Yet taking heart I rose, and then perceiv'd
                    I was deceiv'd:

My hill was further: so I flung away,
                    Yet heard a crie
        Just as I went, *None goes that way*
            And lives: If that be all, said I,
After so foul a journey death is fair,
                    And but a chair.

The Holdfast

I THREATNED to observe the strict decree
        Of my deare God with all my power & might.
        But I was told by one, it could not be;
Yet I might trust in God to be my light.

Then will I trust, said I, in him alone.
    Nay, ev'n to trust in him, was also his:
    We must confesse that nothing is our own.
Then I confesse that he my succour is:
But to have nought is ours, not to confesse
    That we have nought, I stood amaz'd at this,
    Much troubled, till I heard a friend expresse,
That all things were more ours by being his.
    What Adam had, and forfeited for all,
    Christ keepeth now, who cannot fail or fall.

Complaining

Do not beguile my heart,
    Because thou art
My power and wisdome. Put me not to shame,
    Because I am
Thy clay that weeps, thy dust that calls.

Thou art the Lord of glorie;
    The deed and storie
Are both thy due: but I a silly flie,
    That live or die
According as the weather falls.

Art thou all justice, Lord?
    Shows not thy word
More attributes? Am I all throat or eye,
    To weep or crie?
Have I no parts but those of grief?

Let not thy wrathfull power
    Afflict my houre,
My inch of life: or let thy gracious power
    Contract my houre,
That I may climbe and finde relief.

The Discharge

BUSIE enquiring heart, what wouldst thou know?
  Why dost thou prie,
And turn, and leer, and with a licorous eye
  Look high and low;
    And in thy lookings stretch and grow?

Hast thou not made thy counts, and summ'd up all?
  Did not thy heart
Give up the whole, and with the whole depart?
  Let what will fall:
    That which is past who can recall?

Thy life is Gods, thy time to come is gone,
  And is his right.
He is thy night at noon: he is at night
  Thy noon alone.
    The crop is his, for he hath sown.

And well it was for thee, when this befel,
  That God did make
Thy businesse his, and in thy life partake:
  For thou canst tell,
    If it be his once, all is well.

Onely the present is thy part and fee.
  And happy thou,
If, though thou didst not beat thy future brow,
  Thou couldst well see
    What present things requir'd of thee.

They ask enough; why shouldst thou further go?
  Raise not the mudde
Of future depths, but drink the cleare and good.
  Dig not for wo
    In times to come; for it will grow.

Man and the present fit: if he provide,
           He breaks the square.
This houre is mine: if for the next I care,
           I grow too wide,
      And do encroach upon deaths side.

For death each houre environs and surrounds.
           He that would know
And care for future chances, cannot go
           Unto those grounds,
      But through a Church-yard which them bour

Things present shrink and die: but they that spend
           Their thoughts and sense
On future grief, do not remove it thence,
           But it extend,
      And draw the bottome out an end.

God chains the dog till night: wilt loose the chain,
           And wake thy sorrow?
Wilt thou forestall it, and now grieve to morrow,
           And then again
      Grieve over freshly all thy pain?

Either grief will not come: or if it must,
           Do not forecast.
And while it cometh, it is almost past.
           Away distrust:
      My God hath promis'd; he is just.

Praise (II)

KING of Glorie, King of Peace,
           I will love thee:
And that love may never cease,
           I will move thee.

Thou hast granted my request,
   Thou hast heard me:
Thou didst note my working breast,
   Thou hast spar'd me.

Wherefore with my utmost art
   I will sing thee,
And the cream of all my heart
   I will bring thee.

Though my sinnes against me cried,
   Thou didst cleare me;
And alone, when they replied,
   Thou didst heare me.

Sev'n whole dayes, not one in seven,
   I will praise thee.
In my heart, though not in heaven,
   I can raise thee.

Thou grew'st soft and moist with tears,
   Thou relentedst:
And when Justice call'd for fears,
   Thou dissentedst.

Small it is, in this poore sort
   To enroll thee:
Ev'n eternitie is too short
   To extoll thee.

An Offering

COME, bring thy gift. If blessings were as slow
As mens returns, what would become of fools?
What hast thou there? a heart? but is it pure?
Search well and see; for hearts have many holes.
Yet one pure heart is nothing to bestow:
In Christ two natures met to be thy cure.

O that within us hearts had propagation,
Since many gifts do challenge many hearts!
Yet one, if good, may title to a number;
And single things grow fruitfull by deserts.
In publick judgements one may be a nation,
And fence a plague, while others sleep and slumber.

But all I fear is lest thy heart displease,
As neither good, nor one: so oft divisions
Thy lusts have made, and not thy lusts alone;
Thy passions also have their set partitions.
These parcell out thy heart: recover these,
And thou mayst offer many gifts in one.

There is a balsome, or indeed a bloud,
Dropping from heav'n, which doth both cleanse and clos
All sorts of wounds; of such strange force it is.
Seek out this All-heal, and seek no repose,
Untill thou finde and use it to thy good:
Then bring thy gift, and let thy hymne be this;

SINCE my sadnesse
Into gladnesse
Lord thou dost convert,
O accept
What thou hast kept,
As thy due desert.

Had I many,
Had I any,
(For this heart is none)
All were thine
And none of mine:
Surely thine alone.

Yet thy favour
May give savour
To this poore oblation;
And it raise
To be thy praise,
And be my salvation.

Longing

WITH sick and famisht eyes,
With doubling knees and weary bones,
To thee my cries,
To thee my grones,
To thee my sighs, my tears ascend:
No end?

My throat, my soul is hoarse;
My heart is wither'd like a ground
Which thou dost curse.
My thoughts turn round,
And make me giddie; Lord, I fall,
Yet call.

From thee all pitie flows.
Mothers are kinde, because thou art,
And dost dispose
To them a part:
Their infants, them; and they suck thee
More free.

Bowels of pitie, heare!
Lord of my soul, love of my minde,
Bow down thine eare!
Let not the winde
Scatter my words, and in the same
Thy name!

Look on my sorrows round!
Mark well my furnace! O what flames,
    What heats abound!
    What griefs, what shames!
Consider, Lord; Lord, bow thine eare,
      And heare!

Lord Jesu, thou didst bow
Thy dying head upon the tree:
    O be not now
    More dead to me!
Lord heare! *Shall he that made the eare,*
      Not heare?

Behold, thy dust doth stirre,
It moves, it creeps, it aims at thee:
    Wilt thou deferre
    To succour me,
Thy pile of dust, wherein each crumme
      Sayes, Come?

To thee help appertains.
Hast thou left all things to their course,
    And laid the reins
    Upon the horse?
Is all lockt? hath a sinners plea
      No key?

Indeed the world's thy book,
Where all things have their leafe assign'd:
    Yet a meek look
    Hath interlin'd.
Thy board is full, yet humble guests
      Finde nests.

Thou tarriest, while I die,
And fall to nothing: thou dost reigne,
And rule on high,
While I remain
In bitter grief: yet am I stil'd
Thy childe.

Lord, didst thou leave thy throne,
Not to relieve? how can it be,
That thou art grown
Thus hard to me?
Were sinne alive, good cause there were
To bear.

But now both sinne is dead,
And all thy promises live and bide.
That wants his head;
These speak and chide,
And in thy bosome poure my tears,
As theirs.

Lord JESU, heare my heart,
Which hath been broken now so long,
That ev'ry part
Hath got a tongue!
Thy beggars grow; rid them away
To day.

My love, my sweetnesse, heare!
By these thy feet, at which my heart
Lies all the yeare,
Pluck out thy dart,
And heal my troubled breast which cryes,
Which dyes.

The Bag

AWAY despair! my gracious Lord doth heare.
　　Though windes and waves assault my keel,
　　He doth preserve it: he doth steer,
　　Ev'n when the boat seems most to reel.
　　Storms are the triumph of his art:
Well may he close his eyes, but not his heart.

Hast thou not heard, that my Lord JESUS di'd?
　　Then let me tell thee a strange storie.
　　The God of power, as he did ride
　　In his majestick robes of glorie,
　　Resolv'd to light; and so one day
He did descend, undressing all the way.

The starres his tire of light and rings obtain'd,
　　The cloud his bow, the fire his spear,
　　The sky his azure mantle gain'd.
　　And when they ask'd, what he would wear;
　　He smil'd and said as he did go,
He had new clothes a making here below.

When he was come, as travellers are wont,
　　He did repair unto an inne.
　　Both then, and after, many a brunt
　　He did endure to cancell sinne:
　　And having giv'n the rest before,
Here he gave up his life to pay our score.

But as he was returning, there came one
　　That ran upon him with a spear.
　　He, who came hither all alone,
　　Bringing nor man, nor arms, nor fear,
　　Receiv'd the blow upon his side,
And straight he turn'd, and to his brethren cry'd,

If ye have any thing to send or write,
 I have no bag, but here is room:
 Unto my Fathers hands and sight,
 Beleeve me, it shall safely come.
 That I shall minde, what you impart,
Look, you may put it very neare my heart.

Or if hereafter any of my friends
 Will use me in this kinde, the doore
 Shall still be open; what he sends
 I will present, and somewhat more,
 Not to his hurt. Sighs will convey
Any thing to me. Harke, Despair away.

The Jews

 POORE nation, whose sweet sap and juice
Our cyens* have purloin'd, and left you drie:
Whose streams we got by the Apostles sluce,
And use in baptisme, while ye pine and die:
 Who by not keeping once, became a debter;
  And now by keeping lose the letter:

  Oh that my prayers! mine, alas!
Oh that some Angel might a trumpet sound;
At which the Church falling upon her face
Should crie so loud, untill the trump were drown'd,
 And by that crie of her deare Lord obtain,
  That your sweet sap might come again!

The Collar

I STRUCK the board, and cry'd, No more.
  I will abroad.
 What? shall I ever sigh and pine?

* scions

143

My lines and life are free; free as the rode,
　　　Loose as the winde, as large as store.
　　　　　Shall I be still in suit?
　　　　Have I no harvest but a thorn
　　　　To let me bloud, and not restore
　　　What I have lost with cordiall fruit?
　　　　　　　Sure there was wine
Before my sighs did drie it: there was corn
　　　　Before my tears did drown it.
Is the yeare onely lost to me?
　　　　　Have I no bayes to crown it?
No flowers, no garlands gay? all blasted?
　　　　　　All wasted?
　　　Not so, my heart: but there is fruit,
　　　　　And thou hast hands.
　　Recover all thy sigh-blown age
On double pleasures: leave thy cold dispute
Of what is fit, and not. Forsake thy cage,
　　　　　Thy rope of sands,
Which pettie thoughts have made, and made to thee
　　Good cable, to enforce and draw,
　　　　　And be thy law,
　　While thou didst wink and wouldst not see.
　　　　　Away; take heed:
　　　　　I will abroad.
Call in thy deaths head there: tie up thy fears.
　　　　　He that forbears
　　　　To suit and serve his need,
　　　　　Deserves his load.
But as I rav'd and grew more fierce and wilde
　　　　　At every word,
Me thoughts I heard one calling, *Child!*
　　　　And I reply'd, *My Lord.*

144

The Glimpse

WHITHER away delight?
Thou cam'st but now; wilt thou so soon depart,
      And give me up to night?
For many weeks of lingring pain and smart
But one half houre of comfort to my heart?

      Me thinks delight should have
More skill in musick, and keep better time.
      Wert thou a winde or wave,
They quickly go and come with lesser crime:
Flowers look about, and die not in their prime.

      Thy short abode and stay
Feeds not, but addes to the desire of meat.
      Lime begg'd of old, they say,
A neighbour spring to cool his inward heat;
Which by the springs accesse grew much more great.

      In hope of thee my heart
Pickt here and there a crumme, and would not die;
      But constant to his part,
When as my fears foretold this, did replie,
A slender thread a gentle guest will tie.

      Yet if the heart that wept
Must let thee go, return when it doth knock.
      Although thy heap be kept
For future times, the droppings of the stock
May oft break forth, and never break the lock.

      If I have more to spinne,
The wheel shall go, so that thy stay be short.
      Thou knowst how grief and sinne
Disturb the work. O make me not their sport,
Who by thy coming may be made a court!

Assurance

O SPITEFULL bitter thought!
O spitefull thought! Couldst thou invent
So high a torture? Is such poyson bought?
Doubtlesse, but in the way of punishment.
    When wit contrives to meet with thee,
    No such rank poyson can there be.

    Thou said'st but even now,
That all was not so fair, as I conceiv'd,
Betwixt my God and me; that I allow
And coin large hopes, but that I was deceiv'd:
    Either the league was broke, or neare it;
    And, that I had great cause to fear it.

    And what to this? what more
Could poyson, if it had a tongue, expresse?
What is thy aim? wouldst thou unlock the doore
To cold despairs, and gnawing pensivenesse?
    Wouldst thou raise devils? I see, I know,
    I writ thy purpose long ago.

    But I will to my Father,
Who heard thee say it. O most gracious Lord,
If all the hope and comfort that I gather,
Were from my self, I had not half a word,
    Not half a letter to oppose
    What is objected by my foes.

    But thou art my desert:
And in this league, which now my foes invade,
Thou art not onely to perform thy part,
But also mine; as when the league was made
    Thou didst at once thy self indite,
    And hold my hand, while I did write.

Wherefore if thou canst fail,
Then can thy truth and I: but while rocks stand,
And rivers stirre, thou canst not shrink or quail:
Yea, when both rocks and all things shall disband,
    Then shalt thou be my rock and tower,
    And make their ruine praise thy power.

    Now foolish thought go on,
Spin out thy thread, and make thereof a coat
To hide thy shame: for thou hast cast a bone
Which bounds on thee, and will not down thy throat:
    What for it self love once began,
    Now love and truth will end in man.

The Call

COME, my Way, my Truth, my Life:
Such a Way, as gives us breath:
Such a Truth, as ends all strife:
Such a Life, as killeth death.

Come, my Light, my Feast, my Strength:
Such a Light, as shows a feast:
Such a Feast, as mends in length:
Such a Strength, as makes his guest.

Come, my Joy, my Love, my Heart:
Such a Joy, as none can move:
Such a Love, as none can part:
Such a Heart, as joyes in love.

Clasping of hands

LORD, thou art mine, and I am thine,
If mine I am: and thine much more,
Then I or ought, or can be mine.
Yet to be thine, doth me restore;

So that again I now am mine,
And with advantage mine the more,
Since this being mine, brings with it thine,
And thou with me dost thee restore.
    If I without thee would be mine,
    I neither should be mine nor thine.

Lord, I am thine, and thou art mine:
So mine thou art, that something more
I may presume thee mine, then thine.
For thou didst suffer to restore
Not thee, but me, and to be mine,
And with advantage mine the more,
Since thou in death wast none of thine,
Yet then as mine didst me restore.
    O be mine still! still make me thine!
    Or rather make no Thine and Mine!

Praise (III)

LORD, I will mean and speak thy praise,
        Thy praise alone.
My busie heart shall spin it all my dayes:
    And when it stops for want of store,
Then will I wring it with a sigh or grone,
        That thou mayst yet have more.

When thou dost favour any action,
        It runnes, it flies:
All things concurre to give it a perfection.
    That which had but two legs before,
When thou dost blesse, hath twelve: one wheel doth rise
        To twentie then, or more.

But when thou dost on businesse blow,
        It hangs, it clogs:
Not all the teams of Albion in a row
    Can hale or draw it out of doore.
Legs are but stumps, and Pharaohs wheels but logs,
      And struggling hinders more.

Thousands of things do thee employ
        In ruling all
This spacious globe: Angels must have their joy,
    Devils their rod, the sea his shore,
The windes their stint: and yet when I did call,
      Thou heardst my call, and more.

I have not lost one single tear:
         But when mine eyes
Did weep to heav'n, they found a bottle there
    (As we have boxes for the poore)
Readie to take them in; yet of a size
      That would contain much more.

But after thou hadst slipt a drop
        From thy right eye,
(Which there did hang like streamers neare the top
    Of some fair church, to show the sore
And bloudie battell which thou once didst trie)
      The glasse was full and more.

Wherefore I sing. Yet since my heart,
        Though press'd, runnes thin;
O that I might some other hearts convert,
    And so take up at use good store:
That to thy chest there might be coming in
      Both all my praise, and more!

Josephs coat

WOUNDED I sing, tormented I indite,
 Thrown down I fall into a bed, and rest:
Sorrow hath chang'd its note: such is his will,
Who changeth all things, as him pleaseth best.
  For well he knows, if but one grief and smart
Among my many had his full career,
Sure it would carrie with it ev'n my heart,
And both would runne untill they found a biere
  To fetch the bodie; both being due to grief.
But he hath spoil'd the race; and giv'n to anguish
One of Joyes coats, ticing it with relief
To linger in me, and together languish.
  I live to shew his power, who once did bring
My *joyes* to *weep*, and now my *griefs* to *sing*.

The Pulley

WHEN God at first made man,
Having a glasse of blessings standing by;
Let us (said he) poure on him all we can:
Let the worlds riches, which dispersed lie,
  Contract into a span.

So strength first made a way;
Then beautie flow'd, then wisdome, honour, pleasure:
When almost all was out, God made a stay,
Perceiving that alone of all his treasure
  Rest in the bottome lay.

For if I should (said he)
Bestow this jewell also on my creature,
He would adore my gifts in stead of me,
And rest in Nature, not the God of Nature:
  So both should losers be.

Yet let him keep the rest,
But keep them with repining restlesnesse:
Let him be rich and wearie, that at least,
If goodnesse leade him not, yet wearinesse
     May tosse him to my breast.

The Priesthood

BLEST Order, which in power dost so excell,
That with th' one hand thou liftest to the sky,
And with the other throwest down to hell
In thy just censures; fain would I draw nigh,
Fain put thee on, exchanging my lay-sword
     For that of th' holy Word.

But thou art fire, sacred and hallow'd fire;
And I but earth and clay: should I presume
To wear thy habit, the severe attire
My slender compositions might consume.
I am both foul and brittle; much unfit
     To deal in holy Writ.

Yet have I often seen, by cunning hand
And force of fire, what curious things are made
Of wretched earth. Where once I scorn'd to stand,
That earth is fitted by the fire and trade
Of skilfull artists, for the boards of those
     Who make the bravest shows.

But since those great ones, be they ne're so great,
Come from the earth, from whence those vessels come;
So that at once both feeder, dish, and meat
Have one beginning and one finall summe:
I do not greatly wonder at the sight,
     If earth in earth delight.

But th' holy men of God such vessels are,
As serve him up, who all the world commands:
When God vouchsafeth to become our fare,
Their hands convey him, who conveys their hands.
O what pure things, most pure must those things be,
                    Who bring my God to me!

Wherefore I dare not, I, put forth my hand
To hold the Ark, although it seem to shake
Through th' old sinnes and new doctrines of our land.
Onely, since God doth often vessels make
Of lowly matter for high uses meet,
                    I throw me at his feet.

There will I lie, untill my Maker seek
For some mean stuffe whereon to show his skill:
Then is my time. The distance of the meek
Doth flatter power. Lest good come short of ill
In praising might, the poore do by submission
                    What pride by opposition.

The Search

WHITHER, O, whither art thou fled,
                    My Lord, my Love?
My searches are my daily bread;
                    Yet never prove.

My knees pierce th' earth, mine eies the skie;
                    And yet the sphere
And centre-both to me denie
                    That thou art there.

Yet can I mark how herbs below
                    Grow green and gay,
As if to meet thee they did know,
                    While I decay.

Yet can I mark how starres above
        Simper and shine,
As having keyes unto thy love,
        While poore I pine.

I sent a sigh to seek thee out,
        Deep drawn in pain,
Wing'd like an arrow: but my scout
        Returns in vain.

I tun'd another (having store)
        Into a grone;
Because the search was dumbe before:
        But all was one.

Lord, dost thou some new fabrick mould,
        Which favour winnes,
And keeps thee present, leaving th' old
        Unto their sinnes?

Where is my God? what hidden place
        Conceals thee still?
What covert dare eclipse thy face?
        Is it thy will?

O let not that of any thing;
        Let rather brasse,
Or steel, or mountains be thy ring,
        And I will passe.

Thy will such an intrenching is,
        As passeth thought:
To it all strength, all subtilties
        Are things of nought.

Thy will such a strange distance is,
        As that to it
East and West touch, the poles do kisse,
        And parallels meet.

Since then my grief must be as large,
              As is thy space,
Thy distance from me; see my charge,
              Lord, see my case.

O take these barres, these lengths away;
              Turn, and restore me:
Be not Almightie, let me say,
              Against, but for me.

When thou dost turn, and wilt be neare;
              What edge so keen,
What point so piercing can appeare
              To come between?

For as thy absence doth excell
              All distance known:
So doth thy nearenesse bear the bell,
              Making two one.

Grief

O WHO will give me tears? Come all ye springs,
Dwell in my head & eyes: come clouds, & rain:
My grief hath need of all the watry things,
That nature hath produc'd. Let ev'ry vein
Suck up a river to supply mine eyes,
My weary weeping eyes, too drie for me,
Unlesse they get new conduits, new supplies
To bear them out, and with my state agree.
What are two shallow foords, two little spouts
Of a lesse world? the greater is but small,
A narrow cupboard for my griefs and doubts,
Which want provision in the midst of all.

Verses, ye are too fine a thing, too wise
For my rough sorrows: cease, be dumbe and mute,
Give up your feet and running to mine eyes,
And keep your measures for some lovers lute,
Whose grief allows him musick and a ryme:
For mine excludes both measure, tune, and time.
                    Alas, my God!

The Crosse

WHAT is this strange and uncouth thing?
To make me sigh, and seek, and faint, and die,
Untill I had some place, where I might sing,
        And serve thee; and not onely I,
But all my wealth and familie might combine
To set thy honour up, as our designe.

        And then when after much delay,
Much wrastling, many a combate, this deare end,
So much desir'd, is giv'n, to take away
        My power to serve thee; to unbend
All my abilities, my designes confound,
And lay my threatnings bleeding on the ground.

        One ague dwelleth in my bones,
Another in my soul (the memorie
What I would do for thee, if once my grones
        Could be allow'd for harmonie):
I am in all a weak disabled thing,
Save in the sight thereof, where strength doth sting.

        Besides, things sort not to my will,
Ev'n when my will doth studie thy renown:
Thou turnest th' edge of all things on me still,
        Taking me up to throw me down:
So that, ev'n when my hopes seem to be sped,
I am to grief alive, to them as dead.

To have my aim, and yet to be
Further from it then when I bent my bow;
To make my hopes my torture, and the fee
    Of all my woes another wo,
Is in the midst of delicates to need,
And ev'n in Paradise to be a weed.

    Ah my deare Father, ease my smart!
These contrarieties crush me: these crosse actions
Doe winde a rope about, and cut my heart:
    And yet since these thy contradictions
Are properly a crosse felt by thy Sonne,
With but foure words, my words, *Thy will be done*.

The Flower

    How fresh, O Lord, how sweet and clean
Are thy returns! ev'n as the flowers in spring;
    To which, besides their own demean,
The late-past frosts tributes of pleasure bring.
        Grief melts away
        Like snow in May,
As if there were no such cold thing.

    Who would have thought my shrivel'd heart
Could have recover'd greennesse? It was gone
    Quite under ground; as flowers depart
To see their mother-root, when they have blown;
        Where they together
        All the hard weather,
Dead to the world, keep house unknown.

    These are thy wonders, Lord of power,
Killing and quickning, bringing down to hell
    And up to heaven in an houre;
Making a chiming of a passing-bell.

We say amisse,
This or that is:
Thy word is all, if we could spell.

O that I once past changing were,
Fast in thy Paradise, where no flower can wither!
Many a spring I shoot up fair,
Offring at heav'n, growing and groning thither:
Nor doth my flower
Want a spring-showre,
My sinnes and I joining together.

But while I grow in a straight line,
Still upwards bent, as if heav'n were mine own,
Thy anger comes, and I decline:
What frost to that? what pole is not the zone,
Where all things burn,
When thou dost turn,
And the least frown of thine is shown?

And now in age I bud again,
After so many deaths I live and write;
I once more smell the dew and rain,
And relish versing: O my onely light,
It cannot be.
That I am he
On whom thy tempests fell all night.

These are thy wonders, Lord of love,
To make us see we are but flowers that glide:
Which when we once can finde and prove,
Thou hast a garden for us, where to bide.
Who would be more,
Swelling through store,
Forfeit their Paradise by their pride.

Dotage

FALSE glozing pleasures, casks of happinesse,
Foolish night-fires, womens and childrens wishes,
Chases in Arras, guilded emptinesse,
Shadows well mounted, dreams in a career,
Embroider'd lyes, nothing between two dishes;
        These are the pleasures here.

True earnest sorrows, rooted miseries,
Anguish in grain, vexations ripe and blown,
Sure-footed griefs, solid calamities,
Plain demonstrations, evident and cleare,
Fetching their proofs ev'n from the very bone;
        These are the sorrows here.

But oh the folly of distracted men,
Who griefs in earnest, joyes in jest pursue;
Preferring, like brute beasts, a lothsome den
Before a court, ev'n that above so cleare,
Where are no sorrows, but delights more true
        Then miseries are here!

The Sonne

LET forrain nations of their language boast,
What fine varietie each tongue affords:
I like our language, as our men and coast:
Who cannot dresse it well, want wit, not words.
How neatly doe we give one onely name
To parents issue and the sunnes bright starre!
A sonne is light and fruit; a fruitfull flame
Chasing the fathers dimnesse, carri'd farre

From the first man in th' East, to fresh and new
Western discov'ries of posteritie.
So in one word our Lords humilitie
We turn upon him in a sense most true:
 For what Christ once in humblenesse began,
 We him in glorie call, *The Sonne of Man.*

A true Hymne

 My joy, my life, my crown!
 My heart was meaning all the day,
  Somewhat it fain would say:
And still it runneth mutt'ring up and down
With onely this, *My joy, my life, my crown.*

  Yet slight not these few words:
 If truly said, they may take part
  Among the best in art.
The finenesse which a hymne or psalme affords,
Is, when the soul unto the lines accords.

  He who craves all the minde,
 And all the soul, and strength, and time,
  If the words onely ryme,
Justly complains, that somewhat is behinde
To make his verse, or write a hymne in kinde.

  Whereas if th' heart be moved,
 Although the verse be somewhat scant,
  God doth supplie the want.
As when th' heart sayes (sighing to be approved)
O, *could I love!* and stops: God writeth, *Loved.*

The Answer

My comforts drop and melt away like snow:
I shake my head, and all the thoughts and ends,
Which my fierce youth did bandie, fall and flow
Like leaves about me: or like summer friends,
Flyes of estates and sunne-shine. But to all,
Who think me eager, hot, and undertaking,
But in my prosecutions slack and small;
As a young exhalation, newly waking,
Scorns his first bed of dirt, and means the sky;
But cooling by the way, grows pursie and slow,
And setling to a cloud, doth live and die
In that dark state of tears: to all, that so
    Show me, and set me, I have one reply,
    Which they that know the rest, know more then I.

A Dialogue-Antheme

Christian. Death.

Chr.   Alas, poore Death, where is thy glorie?
      Where is thy famous force, thy ancient sting?

Dea.   *Alas poore mortall, void of storie,*
      Go spell and reade how I have kill'd thy King.

Chr.   Poore Death! and who was hurt thereby?
      Thy curse being laid on him, makes thee accurst.

Dea.   *Let losers talk: yet thou shalt die;*
      These arms shall crush thee.

Chr.   Spare not, do thy worst.
    I shall be one day better then before:
    Thou so much worse, that thou shalt be no more.

The Water-course

THOU who dost dwell and linger here below,
Since the condition of this world is frail,
Where of all plants afflictions soonest grow;
If troubles overtake thee, do not wail:

For who can look for lesse, that loveth $\begin{cases} \text{Life?} \\ \text{Strife?} \end{cases}$

But rather turn the pipe and waters course
To serve thy sinnes, and furnish thee with store
Of sov'raigne tears, springing from true remorse:
That so in purenesse thou mayst him adore,

Who gives to man, as he sees fit, $\begin{cases} \text{Salvation.} \\ \text{Damnation.} \end{cases}$

Self-condemnation

THOU who condemnest Jewish hate,
For choosing Barrabas a murderer
    Before the Lord of glorie;
Look back upon thine own estate,
Call home thine eye (that busie wanderer):
    That choice may be thy storie.

He that doth love, and love amisse,
This worlds delights before true Christian joy,
    Hath made a Jewish choice:
The world an ancient murderer is;
Thousands of souls it hath and doth destroy
    With her enchanting voice.

He that hath made a sorrie wedding
Between his soul and gold, and hath preferr'd
    False gain before the true,

Hath done what he condemnes in reading:
For he hath sold for money his deare Lord,
        And is a Judas-Jew.

Thus we prevent the last great day,
And judge our selves. That light, which sin & passion
        Did before dimme and choke,
When once those snuffes are ta'ne away,
Shines bright and cleare, ev'n unto condemnation,
        Without excuse or cloke.

Bitter-sweet

A H my deare angrie Lord,
Since thou dost love, yet strike;
Cast down, yet help afford;
Sure I will do the like.

I will complain, yet praise;
I will bewail, approve:
And all my sowre-sweet dayes
I will lament, and love.

The Glance

W H E N first thy sweet and gracious eye
Vouchsaf'd ev'n in the midst of youth and night
To look upon me, who before did lie
        Weltring in sinne;
I felt a sugred strange delight,
Passing all cordials made by any art,
Bedew, embalme, and overrunne my heart,
        And take it in.

Since that time many a bitter storm
My soul hath felt, ev'n able to destroy,
Had the malicious and ill-meaning harm
      His swing and sway:
But still thy sweet originall joy,
Sprung from thine eye, did work within my soul,
And surging griefs, when they grew bold, controll,
      And got the day.

If thy first glance so powerfull be,
A mirth but open'd and seal'd up again;
What wonders shall we feel, when we shall see
      Thy full-ey'd love!
When thou shalt look us out of pain,
And one aspect of thine spend in delight
More then a thousand sunnes disburse in light,
      In heav'n above.

The 23d Psalme

THE God of love my shepherd is,
      And he that doth me feed:
While he is mine, and I am his,
      What can I want or need?

He leads me to the tender grasse,
      Where I both feed and rest;
Then to the streams that gently passe:
      In both I have the best.

Or if I stray, he doth convert
      And bring my minde in frame:
And all this not for my desert,
      But for his holy name.

Yea, in deaths shadie black abode
　　Well may I walk, not fear:
For thou art with me; and thy rod
　　To guide, thy staffe to bear.

Nay, thou dost make me sit and dine,
　　Ev'n in my enemies sight:
My head with oyl, my cup with wine
　　Runnes over day and night.

Surely thy sweet and wondrous love
　　Shall measure all my dayes;
And as it never shall remove,
　　So neither shall my praise.

Marie Magdalene

WHEN blessed Marie wip'd her Saviours feet,
(Whose precepts she had trampled on before)
And wore them for a jewell on her head,
　　Shewing his steps should be the street,
　　Wherein she thenceforth evermore
With pensive humblenesse would live and tread:

She being stain'd her self, why did she strive
To make him clean, who could not be defil'd?
Why kept she not her tears for her own faults,
　　And not his feet? Though we could dive
　　In tears like seas, our sinnes are pil'd
Deeper then they, in words, and works, and thoughts.

Deare soul, she knew who did vouchsafe and deigne
To bear her filth; and that her sinnes did dash
Ev'n God himself: wherefore she was not loth,
　　As she had brought wherewith to stain,
　　So to bring in wherewith to wash:
And yet in washing one, she washed both.

Aaron

HOLINESSE on the head,
Light and perfections on the breast,
Harmonious bells below, raising the dead
To leade them unto life and rest:
Thus are true Aarons drest.

Profanenesse in my head,
Defects and darknesse in my breast,
A noise of passions ringing me for dead
Unto a place where is no rest:
Poore priest thus am I drest.

Onely another head
I have, another heart and breast,
Another musick, making live not dead,
Without whom I could have no rest:
In him I am well drest.

Christ is my onely head,
My alone onely heart and breast,
My onely musick, striking me ev'n dead;
That to the old man I may rest,
And be in him new drest.

So holy in my head,
Perfect and light in my deare breast,
My doctrine tun'd by Christ, (who is not dead,
But lives in me while I do rest)
Come people; Aaron's drest.

The Odour. 2 Cor. 2. 15

How sweetly doth *My Master* sound! *My Master!*
As Amber-greese leaves a rich sent
Unto the taster:
So do these words a sweet content,
An orientall fragrancie, *My Master.*

With these all day I do perfume my minde,
   My minde ev'n thrust into them both:
     That I might finde
   What cordials make this curious broth,
This broth of smells, that feeds and fats my minde.

My Master, shall I speak? O that to thee
   My servant were a little so,
     As flesh may be;
   That these two words might creep & gro
To some degree of spicinesse to thee!

Then should the Pomander, which was before
   A speaking sweet, mend by reflection,
     And tell me more:
   For pardon of my imperfection
Would warm and work it sweeter then before.

For when *My Master*, which alone is sweet,
   And ev'n in my unworthinesse pleasing,
     Shall call and meet,
   My servant, as thee not displeasing,
That call is but the breathing of the sweet.

This breathing would with gains by sweetning me
   (As sweet things traffick when they meet)
     Return to thee.
   And so this new commerce and sweet
Should all my life employ and busie me.

The Foil

    I F we could see below
The sphere of vertue, and each shining grace
  As plainly as that above doth show;
This were the better skie, the brighter place.

God hath made starres the foil
To set off vertues; griefs to set off sinning:
Yet in this wretched world we toil,
As if grief were not foul, nor vertue winning.

The Forerunners

THE harbingers are come. See, see their mark;
White is their colour, and behold my head.
But must they have my brain? must they dispark
Those sparkling notions, which therein were bred?
Must dulnesse turn me to a clod?
Yet have they left me, *Thou art still my God.*

Good men ye be, to leave me my best room,
Ev'n all my heart, and what is lodged there:
I passe not, I, what of the rest become,
So *Thou art still my God*, be out of fear.
He will be pleased with that dittie;
And if I please him, I write fine and wittie.

Farewell sweet phrases, lovely metaphors.
But will ye leave me thus? when ye before
Of stews and brothels onely knew the doores,
Then did I wash you with my tears, and more,
Brought you to Church well drest and clad:
My God must have my best, ev'n all I had.

Lovely enchanting language, sugar-cane,
Hony of roses, whither wilt thou flie?
Hath some fond lover tic'd thee to thy bane?
And wilt thou leave the Church, and love a stie?
Fie, thou wilt soil thy broider'd coat,
And hurt thy self, and him that sings the note.

Let foolish lovers, if they will love dung,
With canvas, not with arras, clothe their shame:
Let follie speak in her own native tongue.
True beautie dwells on high: ours is a flame
      But borrow'd thence to light us thither.
Beautie and beauteous words should go together.

Yet if you go, I passe not; take your way:
For, *Thou art still my God*, is all that ye
Perhaps with more embellishment can say.
Go birds of spring: let winter have his fee;
      Let a bleak palenesse chalk the doore,
So all within be livelier then before.

The Rose

PRESSE me not to take more pleasure
      In this world of sugred lies,
And to use a larger measure
      Then my strict, yet welcome size.

First, there is no pleasure here:
      Colour'd griefs indeed there are,
Blushing woes, that look as cleare
      As if they could beautie spare.

Or if such deceits there be,
      Such delights I meant to say;
There are no such things to me,
      Who have pass'd my right away.

But I will not much oppose
      Unto what you now advise:
Onely take this gentle rose,
      And therein my answer lies.

What is fairer then a rose?
      What is sweeter? yet it purgeth.
Purgings enmitie disclose,
      Enmitie forbearance urgeth.

If then all that worldlings prize
      Be contracted to a rose;
Sweetly there indeed it lies,
      But it biteth in the close.

So this flower doth judge and sentence
      Worldly joyes to be a scourge:
For they all produce repentance,
      And repentance is a purge.

But I health, not physick choose:
      Onely though I you oppose,
Say that fairly I refuse,
      For my answer is a rose.

Discipline

THROW away thy rod,
Throw away thy wrath:
      O my God,
Take the gentle path.

For my hearts desire
Unto thine is bent:
      I aspire
To a full consent.

Not a word or look
I affect to own,
      But by book,
And thy book alone.

Though I fail, I weep:
Though I halt in pace,
    Yet I creep
To the throne of grace.

Then let wrath remove;
Love will do the deed:
    For with love
Stonie hearts will bleed.

Love is swift of foot;
Love's a man of warre,
    And can shoot,
And can hit from farre.

Who can scape his bow?
That which wrought on thee,
    Brought thee low,
Needs must work on me.

Throw away thy rod;
Though man frailties hath,
    Thou art God:
Throw away thy wrath.

The Invitation

COME ye hither All, whose taste
    Is your waste;
Save your cost, and mend your fare.
God is here prepar'd and drest,
    And the feast,
God, in whom all dainties are.

Come ye hither All, whom wine
    Doth define,
Naming you not to your good:

Weep what ye have drunk amisse,
   And drink this,
Which before ye drink is bloud.

Come ye hither All, whom pain
   Doth arraigne,
Bringing all your sinnes to sight:
Taste and fear not: God is here
   In this cheer,
And on sinne doth cast the fright.

Come ye hither All, whom joy
   Doth destroy,
While ye graze without your bounds:
Here is joy that drowneth quite
   Your delight,
As a floud the lower grounds.

Come ye hither All, whose love
   Is your dove,
And exalts you to the skie:
Here is love, which having breath
   Ev'n in death,
After death can never die.

Lord I have invited all,
   And I shall
Still invite, still call to thee:
For it seems but just and right
   In my sight,
Where is All, there All should be.

The Banquet

WELCOME sweet and sacred cheer,
                    Welcome deare;
With me, in me, live and dwell:
For thy neatnesse passeth sight,
                    Thy delight
Passeth tongue to taste or tell.

O what sweetnesse from the bowl
                    Fills my soul,
Such as is, and makes divine!
Is some starre (fled from the sphere)
                    Melted there,
As we sugar melt in wine?

Or hath sweetnesse in the bread
                    Made a head
To subdue the smell of sinne;
Flowers, and gummes, and powders giving
                    All their living,
Lest the Enemy should winne?

Doubtlesse, neither starre nor flower
                    Hath the power
Such a sweetnesse to impart:
Onely God, who gives perfumes,
                    Flesh assumes,
And with it perfumes my heart.

But as Pomanders and wood
                    Still are good,

Yet being bruis'd are better sented:
God, to show how farre his love
                              Could improve,
Here, as broken, is presented.

When I had forgot my birth,
                              And on earth
In delights of earth was drown'd;
God took bloud, and needs would be
                              Spilt with me,
And so found me on the ground.

Having rais'd me to look up,
                              In a cup
Sweetly he doth meet my taste.
But I still being low and short,
                              Farre from court,
Wine becomes a wing at last.

For with it alone I flie
                              To the skie:
Where I wipe mine eyes, and see
What I seek, for what I sue;
                              Him I view,
Who hath done so much fot me.

Let the wonder of his pitie
                              Be my dittie,
And take up my lines and life:
Hearken under pain of death,
                              Hands and breath;
Strive in this, and love the strife.

The Posie

LET wits contest,
And with their words and posies windows fill:
Lesse then the least
Of all thy mercies, is my posie still.

This on my ring,
This by my picture, in my book I write:
Whether I sing,
Or say, or dictate, this is my delight.

Invention rest,
Comparisons go play, wit use thy will:
Lesse then the least
Of all Gods mercies, is my posie still.

A Parodie

SOULS joy, when thou art gone,
And I alone,
Which cannot be,
Because thou dost abide with me,
And I depend on thee;

Yet when thou dost suppresse
The cheerfulnesse
Of thy abode,
And in my powers not stirre abroad,
But leave me to my load:

O what a damp and shade
Doth me invade!
No stormie night
Can so afflict or so affright,
As thy eclipsed light.

Ah Lord! do not withdraw,
        Lest want of aw
        Make Sinne appeare;
And when thou dost but shine lesse cleare,
    Say, that thou art not here.

And then what life I have,
        While Sinne doth rave,
        And falsly boast,
That I may seek, but thou art lost;
    Thou and alone thou know'st.

O what a deadly cold
        Doth me infold!
        I half beleeve,
That Sinne sayes true: but while I grieve,
    Thou com'st and dost relieve.

The Elixir

TEACH me, my God and King,
In all things thee to see,
And what I do in any thing,
    To do it as for thee:

Not rudely, as a beast,
To runne into an action;
But still to make thee prepossest,
    And give it his perfection.

A man that looks on glasse,
On it may stay his eye;
Or if he pleaseth, through it passe,
    And then the heav'n espie.

All may of thee partake:
    Nothing can be so mean,
Which with his tincture (for thy sake)
    Will not grow bright and clean.

A servant with this clause
    Makes drudgerie divine:
Who sweeps a room, as for thy laws,
    Makes that and th' action fine.

This is the famous stone
    That turneth all to gold:
For that which God doth touch and own
    Cannot for lesse be told.

A Wreath

A WREATHED garland of deserved praise,
Of praise deserved, unto thee I give,
I give to thee, who knowest all my wayes,
My crooked winding wayes, wherein I live,
Wherein I die, not live: for life is straight,
Straight as a line, and ever tends to thee,
To thee, who art more farre above deceit,
Then deceit seems above simplicitie.
Give me simplicitie, that I may live,
So live and like, that I may know, thy wayes,
Know them and practise them: then shall I give
For this poore wreath, give thee a crown of praise.

Death

DEATH, thou wast once an uncouth hideous thing
                    Nothing but bones,
        The sad effect of sadder grones:
Thy mouth was open, but thou couldst not sing.

For we consider'd thee as at some six
            Or ten yeares hence,
      After the losse of life and sense,
Flesh being turn'd to dust, and bones to sticks.

We lookt on this side of thee, shooting short;
            Where we did finde
      The shells of fledge souls left behinde,
Dry dust, which sheds no tears, but may extort.

But since our Saviours death did put some bloud
            Into thy face;
      Thou art grown fair and full of grace,
Much in request, much sought for as a good.

For we do now behold thee gay and glad,
            As at dooms-day;
      When souls shall wear their new aray,
And all thy bones with beautie shall be clad.

Therefore we can go die as sleep, and trust
            Half that we have
      Unto an honest faithfull grave;
Making our pillows either down, or dust.

Dooms-day

        COME away,
      Make no delay.
Summon all the dust to rise,
Till it stirre, and rubbe the eyes;
While this member jogs the other,
Each one whispring, *Live you brother?*

        Come away,
      Make this the day.
Dust, alas, no musick feels,
But thy trumpet: then it kneels,

As peculiar notes and strains
Cure Tarantulas raging pains.

Come away,
O make no stay!
Let the graves make their confession,
Lest at length they plead possession:
Fleshes stubbornnesse may have
Read that lesson to the grave.

Come away,
Thy flock doth stray.
Some to windes their bodie lend,
And in them may drown a friend:
Some in noisome vapours grow
To a plague and publick wo.

Come away,
Help our decay.
Man is out of order hurl'd,
Parcel'd out to all the world.
Lord, thy broken consort raise,
And the musick shall be praise.

Judgement

ALMIGHTIE Judge, how shall poore wretches brook
Thy dreadfull look,
Able a heart of iron to appall,
When thou shalt call
For ev'ry mans peculiar book?

What others mean to do, I know not well;
Yet I heare tell,

That some will turn thee to some leaves therein
            So void of sinne,
   That they in merit shall excell.

But I resolve, when thou shalt call for mine,
            That to decline,
And thrust a Testament into thy hand:
              Let that be scann'd.
   There thou shalt finde my faults are thine.

Heaven

O who will show me those delights on high?
         Echo.   I.
Thou Echo, thou art mortall, all men know.
         Echo.   No.
Wert thou not born among the trees and leaves?
         Echo.   Leaves.
And are there any leaves, that still abide?
         Echo.   Bide.
What leaves are they? impart the matter wholly.
         Echo.   Holy.
Are holy leaves the Echo then of blisse?
         Echo.   Yes.
Then tell me, what is that supreme delight?
         Echo.   Light.
Light to the minde: what shall the will enjoy?
         Echo.   Joy.
But are there cares and businesse with the pleasure?
         Echo.   Leisure.
Light, joy, and leisure; but shall they persever?
         Echo.   Ever.

Love (III)

LOVE bade me welcome: yet my soul drew back,
      Guiltie of dust and sinne.
But quick-ey'd Love, observing me grow slack
      From my first entrance in,
Drew nearer to me, sweetly questioning,
      If I lack'd any thing.

A guest, I answer'd, worthy to be here:
      Love said, You shall be he.
I the unkinde, ungratefull? Ah my deare,
      I cannot look on thee.
Love took my hand, and smiling did reply,
      Who made the eyes but I?

Truth Lord, but I have marr'd them: let my shame
      Go where it doth deserve.
And know you not, sayes Love, who bore the blame?
      My deare, then I will serve.
You must sit down, sayes Love, and taste my meat:
      So I did sit and eat.

FINIS.

Glory be to God on high
And on earth peace
Good will towards men.

THE CHURCH MILITANT

ALMIGHTIE Lord, who from thy glorious throne
Seest and rulest all things ev'n as one:
The smallest ant or atome knows thy power,
Known also to each minute of an houre:
Much more do Common-weals acknowledge thee,
And wrap their policies in thy decree,
Complying with thy counsels, doing nought
Which doth not meet with an eternall thought.
But above all, thy Church and Spouse doth prove
Not the decrees of power, but bands of love.
Early didst thou arise to plant this vine,
Which might the more indeare it to be thine.
Spices come from the East; so did thy Spouse,
Trimme as the light, sweet as the laden boughs
Of *Noahs* shadie vine, chaste as the dove;
Prepar'd and fitted to receive thy love.
The course was westward, that the sunne might light
As well our understanding as our sight.
Where th' Ark did rest, there *Abraham* began
To bring the other Ark from *Canaan*.
Moses pursu'd this: but King *Solomon*
Finish'd and fixt the old religion.
When it grew loose, the Jews did hope in vain
By nailing Christ to fasten it again.
But to the Gentiles he bore crosse and all,
Rending with earthquakes the partition-wall:
Onely whereas the Ark in glorie shone,
Now with the crosse, as with a staffe, alone,
Religion, like a pilgrime, westward bent,
Knocking at all doores, ever as she went.
Yet as the sunne, though forward be his flight,
Listens behinde him, and allows some light,
Till all depart: so went the Church her way,
Letting, while one foot stept, the other stay

Among the eastern nations for a time,
Till both removed to the western clime.
To *Egypt* first she came, where they did prove
Wonders of anger once, but now of love.
The ten Commandments there did flourish more
Then the ten bitter plagues had done before.
Holy *Marcarius* and great *Anthonie*
Made *Pharaoh Moses*, changing th' historie.
Goshen was darknesse, *Egypt* full of lights,
Nilus for monsters brought forth Israelites.
Such power hath mightie Baptisme to produce
For things misshappen, things of highest use.
How deare to me, O God, thy counsels are!
          Who may with thee compare?
Religion thence fled into *Greece*, where arts
Gave her the highest place in all mens hearts.
Learning was pos'd, Philosophie was set,
Sophisters taken in a fishers net.
Plato and *Aristotle* were at a losse,
And wheel'd about again to spell *Christ-Crosse*.
Prayers chas'd syllogismes into their den,
And *Ergo* was transform'd into *Amen*.
Though *Greece* took horse as soon as *Egypt* did,
And *Rome* as both; yet *Egypt* faster rid,
And spent her period and prefixed time
Before the other. *Greece* being past her prime,
Religion went to *Rome*, subduing those,
Who, that they might subdue, made all their foes.
The Warrier his deere skarres no more resounds,
But seems to yeeld Christ hath the greater wounds,
Wounds willingly endur'd to work his blisse,
Who by an ambush lost his Paradise.
The great heart stoops, and taketh from the dust
A sad repentance, not the spoils of lust:
Quitting his spear, lest it should pierce again

Him in his members, who for him was slain.
The Shepherds hook grew to a scepter here,
Giving new names and numbers to the yeare.
But th' Empire dwelt in *Greece*, to comfort them
Who were cut short in *Alexanders* stemme.
In both of these Prowesse and Arts did tame
And tune mens hearts against the Gospel came:
Which using, and not fearing skill in th' one,
Or strength in th' other, did erect her throne.
Many a rent and struggling th' Empire knew,
(As dying things are wont) untill it flew
At length to *Germanie*, still westward bending,
And there the Churches festivall attending:
That as before Empire and Arts made way,
(For no lesse Harbingers would serve then they)
So they might still, and point us out the place
Where first the Church should raise her down-cast face.
Strength levels grounds, Art makes a garden there;
Then showres Religion, and makes all to bear.
Spain in the Empire shar'd with *Germanie*,
But *England* in the higher victorie:
Giving the Church a crown to keep her state,
And not go lesse then she had done of late.
Constantines British line meant this of old,
And did this mysterie wrap up and fold
Within a sheet of paper, which was rent
From times great Chronicle, and hither sent.
Thus both the Church and Sunne together ran
Unto the farthest old meridian.
How deare to me, O God, thy counsels are!
                    Who may with thee compare?
Much about one and the same time and place,
Both where and when the Church began her race,
Sinne did set out of Eastern *Babylon*,
And travell'd westward also: journeying on

He chid the Church away, where e're he came,
Breaking her peace, and tainting her good name.
At first he got to *Egypt*, and did sow
Gardens of gods, which ev'ry yeare did grow
Fresh and fine deities. They were at great cost,
Who for a god clearly a sallet lost.
Ah, what a thing is man devoid of grace,
Adoring garlick with an humble face,
Begging his food of that which he may eat,
Starving the while he worshippeth his meat!
Who makes a root his god, how low is he,
If God and man be sever'd infinitely!
What wretchednesse can give him any room,
Whose house is foul, while he adores his broom?
None will beleeve this now, though money be
In us the same transplanted foolerie.
Thus Sinne in *Egypt* sneaked for a while;
His highest was an ox or crocodile,
And such poore game. Thence he to *Greece* doth passe
And being craftier much then Goodnesse was,
He left behinde him garrisons of sinnes
To make good that which ev'ry day he winnes.
Here Sinne took heart, and for a garden-bed
Rich shrines and oracles he purchased:
He grew a gallant, and would needs foretell
As well what should befall, as what befell.
Nay, he became a poet, and would serve
His pills of sublimate in that conserve.
The world came in with hands and purses full
To this great lotterie, and all would pull.
But all was glorious cheating, brave deceit,
Where some poore truths were shuffled for a bait
To credit him, and to discredit those
Who after him should braver truths disclose.
From *Greece* he went to *Rome*: and as before

He was a God, now he's an Emperour.
Nero and others lodg'd him bravely there,
Put him in trust to rule the Roman sphere.
Glorie was his chief instrument of old:
Pleasure succeeded straight, when that grew cold.
Which soon was blown to such a mightie flame,
That though our Saviour did destroy the game,
Disparking oracles, and all their treasure,
Setting affliction to encounter pleasure;
Yet did a rogue with hope of carnall joy
Cheat the most subtill nations. Who so coy,
So trimme, as *Greece* and *Egypt*? yet their hearts
Are given over, for their curious arts,
To such Mahometan stupidities,
As the old heathen would deem prodigies.
How deare to me, O God, thy counsels are!
                    Who may with thee compare?
Onely the West and *Rome* do keep them free
From this contagious infidelitie.
And this is all the Rock, whereof they boast,
As *Rome* will one day finde unto her cost.
Sinne being not able to extirpate quite
The Churches here, bravely resolv'd one night
To be a Church-man too, and wear a Mitre:
The old debauched ruffian would turn writer.
I saw him in his studie, where he sate
Busie in controversies sprung of late.
A gown and pen became him wondrous well:
His grave aspect had more of heav'n then hell:
Onely there was a handsome picture by,
To which he lent a corner of his eye.
As Sinne in *Greece* a Prophet was before,
And in old *Rome* a mightie Emperour;
So now being Priest he plainly did professe
To make a jest of Christs three offices:

The rather since his scatter'd jugglings were
United now in one both time and sphere.
From *Egypt* he took pettie deities,
From *Greece* oracular infallibilities,
And from old *Rome* the libertie of pleasure
By free dispensings of the Churches treasure.
Then in memoriall of his ancient throne
He did surname his palace, *Babylon.*
Yet that he might the better gain all nations,
And make that name good by their transmigrations,
From all these places, but at divers times,
He took fine vizards to conceal his crimes:
From *Egypt* Anchorisme and retirednesse,
Learning from *Greece,* from old *Rome* statelinesse:
And blending these he carri'd all mens eyes,
While Truth sat by, counting his victories:
Whereby he grew apace and scorn'd to use
Such force as once did captivate the Jews;
But did bewitch, and finely work each nation
Into a voluntarie transmigration.
All poste to *Rome:* Princes submit their necks
Either t' his publick foot or private tricks.
It did not fit his gravitie to stirre,
Nor his long journey, nor his gout and furre.
Therefore he sent out able ministers,
Statesmen within, without doores cloisterers:
Who without spear, or sword, or other drumme
Then what was in their tongue, did overcome;
And having conquer'd, did so strangely rule,
That the whole world did seem but the Popes mule.
As new and old *Rome* did one Empire twist;
So both together are one Antichrist,
Yet with two faces, as their *Janus* was,
Being in this their old crackt looking-glasse.
How deare to me, O God, thy counsels are!

Who may with thee compare?

Thus Sinne triumphs in Western *Babylon*;
Yet not as Sinne, but as Religion.
Of his two thrones he made the latter best,
And to defray his journey from the east.
Old and new *Babylon* are to hell and night,
As is the moon and sunne to heav'n and light.
When th' one did set, the other did take place,
Confronting equally the Law and Grace.
They are hells land-marks, Satans double crest:
They are Sinnes nipples, feeding th' east and west.
But as in vice the copie still exceeds
The pattern, but not so in vertuous deeds;
So though Sinne made his latter seat the better,
The latter Church is to the first a debter.
The second Temple could not reach the first:
And the late reformation never durst
Compare with ancient times and purer yeares;
But in the Jews and us deserveth tears.
Nay, it shall ev'ry yeare decrease and fade;
Till such a darknesse do the world invade
At Christs last coming, as his first did finde:
Yet must there such proportion be assign'd
To these diminishings, as is between
The spacious world and *Jurie* to be seen.
Religion stands on tip-toe in our land,
Readie to passe to the *American* strand.
When height of malice, and prodigious lusts,
Impudent sinning, witchcrafts, and distrusts
(The marks of future bane) shall fill our cup
Unto the brimme, and make our measure up;
When *Sein* shall swallow *Tiber*, and the *Thames*
By letting in them both pollutes her streams:
When *Italie* of us shall have her will,
And all her calender of sinnes fulfill;

Whereby one may foretell, what sinnes next yeare
Shall both in *France* and *England* domineer:
Then shall Religion to *America* flee:
They have their times of Gospel, ev'n as we.
My God, thou dost prepare for them a way
By carrying first their gold from them away:
For gold and grace did never yet agree:
Religion alwaies sides with povertie.
We think we rob them, but we think amisse:
We are more poore, and they more rich by this.
Thou wilt revenge their quarrell, making grace
To pay our debts, and leave her ancient place
To go to them, while that which now their nation
But lends to us, shall be our desolation.
Yet as the Church shall thither westward flie,
So Sinne shall trace and dog her instantly:
They have their period also and set times
Both for their vertuous actions and their crimes.
And where of old the Empire and the Arts
Usher'd the Gospel ever in mens hearts,
Spain hath done one; when Arts perform the other,
The Church shall come, & Sinne the Church shall smother:
That when they have accomplished their round,
And met in th' east their first and ancient sound,
Judgement may meet them both & search them round.
Thus do both lights, as well in Church as Sunne,
Light one another, and together runne.
Thus also Sinne and Darknesse follow still
The Church and Sunne with all their power and skill.
But as the Sunne still goes both west and east;
So also did the Church by going west
Still eastward go; because it drew more neare
To time and place, where judgements shall appeare.
How deare to me, O God, thy counsels are!
                    Who may with thee compare?

L'Envoy

King of Glorie, King of Peace,
With the one make warre to cease;
With the other blesse thy sheep,
Thee to love, in thee to sleep.
Let not Sinne devoure thy fold,
Bragging that thy bloud is cold,
That thy death is also dead,
While his conquests dayly spread;
That thy flesh hath lost his food,
And thy Crosse is common wood.
Choke him, let him say no more,
But reserve his breath in store,
Till thy conquests and his fall
Make his sighs to use it all,
And then bargain with the winde
To discharge what is behinde.

Blessed be God *alone,*
Thrice blessed Three in One.

FINIS.

ENGLISH POEMS IN THE WILLIAMS MS. NOT INCLUDED IN *THE TEMPLE*

1. *The H. Communion*

O GRATIOUS Lord, how shall I know
Whether in these gifts thou bee so
   As thou art evry where;
Or rather so, as thou alone
Tak'st all the Lodging, leaving none
   ffor thy poore creature there?

ffirst I am sure, whether bread stay
Or whether Bread doe fly away
   Concerneth bread, not mee.
But that both thou and all thy traine
Bee there, to thy truth, & my gaine,
   Concerneth mee & Thee.

And if in comming to thy foes
Thou dost come first to them, that showes
   The hast of thy good will.
Or if that thou two stations makest
In Bread & mee, the way thou takest
   Is more, but for mee still.

Then of this also I am sure
That thou didst all those pains endure
   To' abolish Sinn, not Wheat.
Creatures are good, & have their place;
Sinn onely, which did all deface,
   Thou drivest from his seat.

I could beleeue an Impanation
At the rate of an Incarnation,
   If thou hadst dyde for Bread.
But that which made my soule to dye,
My flesh, & fleshly villany,
   That allso made thee dead.

That fflesh is there, mine eyes deny:
And what shold flesh but flesh discry,
   The noblest sence of five?
If glorious bodies pass the sight,
Shall they be food & strength & might
   Euen there, where they deceiue?

Into my soule this cannot pass;
fflesh (though exalted) keeps his grass
   And cannot turn to soule.
Bodyes & Minds are different Spheres,
Nor can they change their bounds & meres,
   But keep a constant Pole.

This gift of all gifts is the best,
Thy flesh the least that I request.
   Thou took'st that pledg from mee:
Give me not that I had before,
Or give mee that, so I have more;
   My God, give mee all Thee.

II. *Love*

THOU art too hard for me in Love:
There is no dealing with thee in that Art:
   That is thy Master-peece I see.
  When I contrive & plott to prove
Something that may be conquest on my part,
   Thou Still, O Lord, outstripest mee.

Sometimes, when as I wash, I say,
And shrodely, as I think, Lord wash my soule
    More spotted then my flesh can bee.
    But then there comes into my way
Thy ancient baptism, which when I was foule
    And knew it not, yet cleansed mee.

I took a time when thou didst sleep,
Great waves of trouble combating my brest:
    I thought it braue to praise thee then,
    Yet then I found, that thou didst creep
Into my hart with ioye, giving more rest
    Then flesh did lend thee back agen.

Let mee but once the conquest have
Vpon the matter, 'twill thy conquest prove:
    If thou subdue mortalitie,
    Thou do'st no more then doth the graue:
Whereas if I orecome thee & thy Love,
    Hell, Death & Divel come short of mee.

III. *Trinity Sunday*

HE that is one,
Is none.
Two reacheth thee
In some degree.
Nature & Grace
With Glory may attaine thy Face.
    Steele & a flint strike fire,
        Witt & desire
    Never to thee aspire,
Except life catch & hold those fast.
        That which beleefe
Did not confess in the first Theefe

His fall can tell,
ffrom Heaven, through Earth, to Hell.
Lett two of those alone
To them that fall,
Who God & Saints and Angels loose at last.
Hee that has one,
Has all.

IV. *Euen-song*

THE Day is spent, & hath his will on mee:
  I and the Sunn haue runn our races,
  I went the slower, yet more paces,
    ffor I decay, not hee.

Lord make my Losses vp, & sett mee free:
  That I who cannot now by day
  Look on his daring brightnes, may
    Shine then more bright then hee.

If thou deferr this light, then shadow mee:
  Least that the Night, earths gloomy shade,
  ffouling her nest, my earth invade,
    As if shades knew not Thee.

But thou art Light & darknes both togeather:
  If that bee dark we can not see,
  The sunn is darker then a Tree,
    And thou more dark then either.

Yet Thou art not so dark, since I know this,
  But that my darknes may touch thine,
  And hope, that may teach it to shine,
    Since Light thy Darknes is.

O lett my Soule, whose keyes I must deliver
    Into the hands of senceles Dreames
    Which know not thee, suck in thy beames
      And wake with thee for ever.

v. *The Knell*

    THE Bell doth tolle:
Lord help thy servant whose perplexed Soule
    Doth wishly look
    On either hand
And sometimes offers, sometimes makes a stand,
    Strugling on th' hook.

    Now is the season,
Now the great combat of our flesh & reason:
    O help, my God!
    See, they breake in,
Disbanded humours, sorrows, troops of Sinn,
    Each with his rodd.

    Lord make thy Blood
Convert & colour all the other flood
    And streams of grief,
    That they may bee
Julips & Cordials when wee call on thee
    ffor some relief.

vi. *Perseverance*

MY God, the poore expressions of my Love
Which warme these lines & serve them vp to thee
Are so, as for the present I did moue,
    Or rather as thou mouedst mee.

But what shall issue, whither these my words
Shal help another, but my iudgment bee,
As a burst fouling-peece doth saue the birds
   But kill the man, is seald with thee.

ffor who can tell, though thou hast dyde to winn
And wedd my soule in glorious paradise,
Whither my many crymes and vse of sinn
   May yet forbid the banes and bliss?

Onely my soule hangs on thy promisses
With face and hands clinging vnto thy brest,
Clinging and crying, crying without cease,
   Thou art my rock, thou art my rest.

POEMS FROM WALTON'S
LIVES

Sonnets

My God, where is that ancient heat towards thee,
   Wherewith whole showls of *Martyrs* once did burn,
   Besides their other flames? Doth Poetry
Wear *Venus* Livery? only serve her turn?
Why are not *Sonnets* made of thee? and layes
   Upon thine Altar burnt? Cannot thy love
   Heighten a spirit to sound out thy praise
As well as any she? Cannot thy *Dove*
Out-strip their *Cupid* easily in flight?
   Or, since thy wayes are deep, and still the same,
   Will not a verse run smooth that bears thy name?
Why doth that fire, which by thy power and might
   Each breast does feel, no braver fuel choose
   Than that, which one day Worms may chance refuse?

    Sure, Lord, there is enough in thee to dry
      Oceans of *Ink*; for, as the Deluge did
      Cover the Earth, so doth thy Majesty:
    Each Cloud distills thy praise, and doth forbid
    Poets to turn it to another use.
      Roses and *Lillies* speak thee; and to make
      A pair of Cheeks of them, is thy abuse.
    Why should I *Womens eyes* for Chrystal take?
    Such poor invention burns in their low mind
      Whose fire is wild, and doth not upward go
      To praise, and on thee, Lord, some *Ink* bestow.
    Open the bones, and you shall nothing find
      In the best *face* but *filth*, when, Lord, in thee
      The *beauty* lies in the *discovery*.

To my Successor

IF thou chance for to find
A new House to thy mind,
And built without thy Cost:
Be good to the Poor,
As God gives thee store,
And then, my Labour's not lost.

Another version

IF thou dost find an house built to thy mind
Without thy cost,
Serve thou the more God and the poore;
My labour is not lost.

DOUBTFUL POEMS

On Sir John Danvers

PASSE not by,
Search and you may
Find a treasure
Worth your stay.
What makes a Danvers
Would you find?
In a fayre bodie
A fayre mind.

Sr John Danvers' earthly part
Here is copied out by art;
But his heavenly and divine,
In his progenie doth shine.
Had he only brought them forth,
Know that much had been his worth;
There's no monument to a sonne,
Reade him there, and I have done.

On Henry Danvers earl of Danby

EPITAPH

SACRED Marble, safely keepe
His dvst who vnder thee must sleepe
Vntill the graues againe restore
Theire dead, and Time shalbe no more:
Meane while, if hee (wch all thinges weares)
Doe ruine thee; or if the teares

Are shed for him, dissolve thy frame,
Thov art reqvited; for his Fame,
His Vertves, and his Worth shalbee
Another Monvment for Thee.

G: HERBERᵀ:

To the Right Hon. the L. Chancellor (Bacon

MY Lord. A diamond to mee you sent,
And I to you a Blackamore present.
Gifts speake their Giuers. For as thóse Refractions,
Shining and sharp, point out your rare Perfections;
So by the Other, you may read in mee
(Whom Schollers Habitt, & Obscurity
Hath soild with Black) the colour of my state,
Till your bright gift my darknesse did abate.
Onely, most noble Lord, shutt not the doore
Against this meane & humble Blackamore.
    Perhaps some other subiect I had tryed
    But that my Inke was factious for this side.

A Paradox

That the Sicke are in better State then the Whole

YOU whoe admire yourselues because
    You neither groane nor weepe
And thinke it contrary to Natures Lawes
    To want one ownce of sleepe,
        Your stronge beilefe
Acquitts yourselues and giues the sicke all greife.

Your state, to ours, is contrary;
    That makes you thinke us poore:

So Blackamoores repute us fowle, and wee
    Are quit with them and more.
            Nothinge can see
And iudge of things but Mediocritie.

    The sicke are in themselues a State
        Wheare health hath nought to doe;
How know you that our teares proceed from woe
        And not from better ffate,
            Since that mirth hath
Hir waters alsoe and desired Bathe.

    How know you that the sighes we send
        From wante of breath proceede,
Not from excesse, and therefore doe we spende
        That which wee doe not neede:
            So tremblinge may
As well show inward warblinge as decay.

    Cease then to iudge calamityes
        By outward forme and showe,
But veywe yourselues, & inward turn your eyes;
        Then you shall fully knowe
            That your estate
Is of the two the far more desperate.

    You allwayes feare to feele those smarts
        Which wee but somtymes proue:
Each little comforte much affects our hartes,
        None but gross ioyes you moue:
            Why then confesse
Your feares in number more, your ioyes are lesse.

    Then for yourselues not us embrace
        Playntes to bad fortunes dew:
For though you vysit us, & wayle our case,

Wee doubt much whether you
Come to our bed
To comforte us, or to bee comforted.

To the Queene of Bohemia

BRIGHT soule, of whome if any countrey knowne
Worthy had bin, thou hadst not lost thine owne:
No Earth can bee thy Jointure. For the sunne
And starres alone vnto the pitch doe runne
And pace of thy swift vertues; onely they
Are thy dominion. Those that rule in clay
Stick fast therein, but thy transcendent soule
Doth for two clods of earth ten spheres controule,
And though starres shott from heauen loose their ligh
Yet thy braue beames excluded from their right
Maintaine there Lustre still, & shining cleere
Turne watrish Holland to a chrystalline sphere.
Mee thinkes, in that Dutch optick I doe see
Thy curious vertues much more visibly:
There is thy best Throne. For afflictions are
A foile to sett of worth, & make it rare.
Through that black tiffany thy vertues shine
Fairer & richer. Now wee know, what's thine,
And what is fortunes. Thou hast singled out
Sorrowes & griefs, to fight with them a bout
At there owne weapons, without pomp or state
To second thee against there cunning hate.
O what a poore thing 'tis to bee a Queene
When scepters, state, Attendants are the screen
Betwixt us & the people: when as glory
Lyes round about us to helpe out the story,
When all things pull & hale, that they may bring
A slow behauiour to the style of king,

When sense is made by Comments. But that face
Whose natiue beauty needs not dresse or lace
To serue it forth, & being stript of all
Is selfe-sufficient to bee the thrall
Of thousand harts: that face doth figure thee
And show thy vndiuided Maiestye
Which misery cannot vntwist but rather
Addes to the vnion, as lights doe gather
Splendour from darknes. So close sits the crowne
About thy temples that the furious frowne
Of opposition cannot place thee, where
Thou shalt not bee a Queene and conquer there.

 Yet hast thou more dominions: God doth giue
Children for kingdomes to thee; they shall liue
To conquere new ones, & shall share the frame
Of th' vniuerse, like as the windes, & name
The world anew: the sunne shall neuer rise
But it shall spy some of there victories.
There hands shall clipp the Eagles winges, & chase
Those rauening Harpyes, which peck at thy face,
At once to Hell, without a baiting while
At Purgatory, there inchanted Ile,
And Paris garden. Then let there perfume
And Spanish sents, wisely layd vp, presume
To deale with brimstone, that vntamed stench
Whose fier, like there malice, nought can quench.

 But ioyes are stord for thee: thou shalt returne
Laden with comforts thence, where now to morne
Is thy chief gouernment, to manage woe,
To curbe some Rebell teares, which faine would flow,
Making a Head & spring against thy Reason.
This is thy empire yet: till better season
Call thee from out of that surrounded land,
That habitable sea, & brinish strand,
Thy teares not needing. For that hand Diuine

Which mingles water with thy Rhenish wine
Will pour full ioyes to thee, but dregs to those,
And meet theire tast, who are thy bitter foes.

L'Envoy

SHINE on, Maiestick soule, abide
Like Dauid's tree, planted beside
The Flemmish riuers: in the end
Thy fruite shall with there drops contend;
Great God will surely dry those teares,
Which now that moist land to thee beares.
Then shall thy Glory, fresh as flowers
In water kept, maugre the powers
Of Diuell, Jessuitt & Spaine,
From Holland saile into the Maine:
Thence wheeling on, it compass shall
This oure great Sublunary Ball,
And with that Ring thy fame shall wedd
Eternity into one Bedd.

The Convert

AN ODE

IF ever Tears did flow from *Eyes*,
If ever *Voice* was hoarse with Cries,
If ever *Heart* was sore with Sighs;
  Let now my *Eyes*, my *Voice*, my *Heart*,
  Strive each to play their Part.

My *Eyes*, from whence these Tears did spring,
Where treach'rous Syrens us'd to sing,
Shall flow no more—until they bring

  A Deluge on my sensual Flame,
    And wash away my Shame.

My *Voice*, that oft with foolish Lays,
With Vows and Rants, and sensless Praise,
Frail Beauty's Charms to Heav'n did raise,
  Henceforth shall only pierce the Skies,
    In Penitential Cryes.

My *Heart*, that gave fond Thoughts their Food,
(Till now averse to all that's Good)
The Temple where an *Idol* stood,
  Henceforth in Sacred Flames shall Burn,
    And be that *Idol's* URN.

PSALMS

Psalm 1

  BLEST is the man that never would
    in councels of th' ungodly share,
  Nor hath in way of sinners stood,
    nor sitten in the scorners chair.

  But in God's Law sets his delight,
    and makes that law alone to be
  His meditation day and night:
    he shall be like an happy tree,

  Which, planted by the waters, shall
    with timely fruit still laden stand:
  His leaf shall never fade, and all
    shall prosper that he takes in hand.

The wicked are not so, but they
    are like the chaff, which from the face
Of earth is driven by winds away,
    and finds no sure abiding place.

Therefore shall not the wicked be
    able to stand the Judges doom:
Nor in the safe society
    of good men shall the wicked come.

For God himself vouchsafes to know
    the way that right'ous men have gone:
And those wayes which the wicked go
    shall utterly be overthrown.

Psalm II

WHY are the *Heathen* swell'd with rage,
    the people vain exploits devise?
The Kings and Potentates of earth
    combin'd in one great faction rise.

And taking councels 'gainst the Lord,
    and 'gainst his *Christ*, presume to say,
Let us in sunder break their bonds,
    and from us cast their cords away.

But He, that sits in Heaven, shall laugh,
    the Lord himself shall them deride:
Then shall He speak to them in wrath,
    and in sore anger vex their pride.

But I by God am seated King,
    on *Sion* His most Holy hill,
I will declare the Lords decree,
    nor can I hide his sacred will.

He said to me, Thou art my Son,
   this day have I begotten thee:
Make thy request, and I will grant
   the *Heathen* shall thy portion be.

Thou shalt possess earth's farthest bounds
   and there an awful Scepter sway:
Whose pow'r shall dash and break them all
   like vessels made of brittle clay.

Now therefore, O ye Kings, be wise,
   be learned, ye that judge the earth:
Serve our great God in fear, rejoyce,
   but tremble in your highest mirth.

O kiss the Son, lest he be wrath,
   and straight ye perish from the way:
When once his anger burns, thrice blest
   are all that make the Son their stay.

Psalm III

How are my foes increased, Lord?
   many are they that rise
Against me, saying, For my soul
   no help in God there is.
But thou, O Lord, art still the shield
   of my deliverance:
Thou art my glory, Lord, and he
   that doth my head advance.

I cry'd unto the Lord, he heard
   me from his holy hill:
I laid me down and slept, I wak'd;
   for God sustain'd me still.

Aided by him, I will not fear
    ten thousand enemies:
Nor all the people round about,
    that can against me rise.

Arise, O Lord, and rescue me;
    save me, my God, from thrall:
For thou upon the cheek-bone smit'st
    mine adversaries all.
And thou hast brok th' *ungodly's* teeth:
    Salvation unto thee
Belongs, O Lord, thy blessing shall
    upon thy people be.

Psalm IV

LORD hear me when I call on Thee,
    Lord of my righteousness:
O thou that hast enlarged me
    when I was in distress.

Have mercy on me Lord, and hear
    the Prayer that I frame:
How long will ye, vain men, convert
    my glory into shame?

How long will ye seek after lies,
    and vanity approve?
But know the Lord himself doth chuse
    the righteous man to love.

The Lord will harken unto me
    when I his grace implore:
O learn to stand in awe of him,
    and sin not any more.

Within your chamber try your hearts,
   offer to God on high
The sacrifice of righteousness,
   and on his grace rely.

Many there are that say, O who
   will shew us good? But, Lord,
Thy countenances cheering light
   do thou to us afford.

For that, O Lord, with perfect joy
   shall more replenish me,
Then wordlings joy'd with all their store
   of corn and wine can be.

Therefore will I lie down in peace,
   and take my restful sleep:
For thy protection, Lord, alone
   shall me in safety keep.

Psalm V

LORD to my words encline thine ear,
   my meditation weigh:
My King, my God, vouchsafe to hear
   my cry to thee, I pray.

Thou in the morn shalt have my mone,
   for in the morn will I
Direct my prayers to thy Throne,
   and thither lift mine eye.

Thou art a God whose puritie
   cannot in sins delight:
No evil, Lord, shall dwell with thee,
   nor fools stand in thy sight.

Thou hat'st those that unjustly do:
  thou slay'st the men that lye:
The bloody man, the false one too,
  shall be abhorr'd by thee.

But in th' abundance of thy Grace
  will I to thee draw near:
And toward thy most Holy place
  will worship thee in fear.

Lord lead me in thy righteousness,
  because of all my foes:
And to my dym and sinful eyes
  thy perfect way disclose.

For wickedness their insides are,
  their mouths no truth retain.
Their throat an open Sepulcher,
  their flattering tongues do fain.

Destroy them, Lord, and by their own
  bad councels let them fall:
In hight of their transgression,
  ô Lord, reject them all,

Because against thy Majesty
  they vainly have rebell'd:
But let all those that trust in thee
  with perfect joy be fill'd.

Yea, shout for joy for evermore,
  protected still by thee:
Let them that do thy name adore
  in that still joyful bee.

For God doth righteous men esteem,
   and them for ever bless.
His favour shall encompass them,
   a shield in their distress.

Psalm VI

REBUKE me not in wrath, O Lord,
   nor in thine anger chasten me:
O pity me! for I (O Lord)
   am nothing but Infirmitie.

O heal me, for my bones are vex'd,
   my Soul is troubled very sore;
But, Lord, how long so much perplex'd
   shall I in vain thy Grace implore?

Return, O God! and rescue me,
   my Soul for thy great mercy save;
For who in death remember Thee?
   or who shall praise Thee in the grave?

With groaning I am wearied,
   all night I make my Couch to swim;
And water with salt tears my Bed,
   my sight with sorrow waxeth dim.

My beauty wears and doth decay
   because of all mine Enemies;
But now from me depart away,
   all ye that work Iniquities.

For God himself hath heard my cry;
   the Lord vouchsafes to weigh my tears
Yea, he my prayer from on high
   and humble supplication hears.

And now my foes the Lord will blame
    that er'st so sorely vexed me,
And put them all to utter shame,
    and to confusion suddainly.

Psalm VII

SAVE me, my Lord, my God, because
    I put my trust in Thee:
From all that persecute my life,
    O Lord deliver mee!

Lest like a Lion swollen with rage
    he do devour my soul:
And peace-meal rent it, while there's none
    his mallice to controul.

If I have done this thing, O Lord,
    if I so guilty be:
If I have ill rewarded him
    that was at peace with me:

Yea, have not oft deliver'd him
    that was my causeless foe:
Then let mine enemie prevail
    unto mine overthrow.

Let him pursue and take my soul,
    yea, let him to the Clay
Tread down my life, and in the dust
    my slaughter'd honour lay.

Arise in wrath, O Lord, advance
    against my foes disdain:
Wake and confirm that judgment now,
    which Thou did'st preordain.

So shall the people round about
    resort to give Thee praise;
For their sakes, Lord, return on high,
    and high thy Glory raise.

The Lord shall judge the people all:
    O God consider me
According to my righteousness,
    and mine integritie!

The wicked's malice, Lord, confound,
    but just men ever guide:
Thou art that righteous God by whom
    the hearts and reins are try'd.

God is my shield, who doth preserve
    those that in heart are right:
He judgeth both the good, and those
    that do his justice slight.

Unless the wicked turn again,
    the Lord will whet his Sword:
His bow is bent, his quiver is
    with shafts of vengeance stor'd.

The fatal instruments of death
    in that prepared be:
His arrows are ordain'd 'gainst him
    that persecuteth me.

Behold, the wicked travelleth
    with his iniquitie:
Exploits of mischief he conceives,
    but shall bring forth a lye.

The wicked digged, and a pit
    for others ruine wrought:
But in the pit which he hath made
    shall he himself be caught.

To his own head his wickedness
    shall be returned home:
And on his own accursed pate
    his cruelty shall come.

But I for all his righteousness
    the Lord will magnifie:
And ever praise the Glorious name
    of him that is on high.

GEORGII HERBERTI ANGLI

MVSAE RESPONSORIAE

AD ANDREAE MELVINI SCOTI
ANTI·TAMI·CAMI·CATEGORIAM

Augustissimo Potentissimóque Monarchae

IACOBO, D.G.

Magnae Britanniae, Franciae, & Hiberniae
Regi, Fidei Defensori &c.
Geo. Herbertus

Ecce recedentis foecundo in littore Nili
  Sol generat populum luce fouente nouum.
Antè tui, *CAESAR*, quàm fulserat aura fauoris,
  Nostrae etiam Musae vile fuere lutum:
Nunc adeò per te viuunt, vt repere possint,
  Síntque ausae thalamum solis adire tui.

Illustriss. Celsissimóque
CAROLO
Walliae, & Iuuentutis Principi

Qvam chartam tibi porrigo recentem,
Humanae decus atque apex iuuentae,
Obtutu placido benignus affles,
Namque aspectibus è tuis vel vnus

215

Mordaces tineas, nigrásque blattas,
Quas liuor mihi parturit, retundet,
Ceu, quas culta timet seges, pruinas
Nascentes radij fugant, vel acres
Tantùm dulcia leniunt catarrhos.
Sic o te (iuuenem, senémue) credat
Mors semper iuuenem, senem Britanni.

Reuerendissimo in Christo Patri ac Domino, EPISCOPO VINTONIENSI, &c.

SANCTE Pater, coeli custos, quo doctius vno
Terra nihil, nec quo sanctius astra vident;
Cùm mea futilibus numeris se verba viderent
Claudi, penè tuas praeteriêre fores.
Sed properè dextréque reduxit euntia sensus,
Ista docens soli scripta quadrare tibi.

PRO DISCIPLINA ECCLESIAE NOSTRAE EPIGRAMMATA APOLOGETICA

1. Ad Regem

Instituti Epigrammatici ratio

CVM millena tuam pulsare negotia mentem
Constet, & ex illâ pendeat orbis ope;
Ne te productis videar lassare Camoenis,
Pro solido, CAESAR, carmine frusta dabo.
Cùm tu contundis Catharos, vultúque librísque,
Grata mihi mensae sunt analecta tuae.

II. Ad Melvinum

Non mea fert aetas, vt te, veterane, lacessam;
  Non vt te superem: res tamen ipsa feret.
Aetatis numerum supplebit causa minorem:
  Sic tu nunc iuuenis factus, egóque senex.
Aspice, dum perstas, vt te tua deserat aetas,
  Et mea sint canis scripta referta tuis.
Ecce tamen quàm suauis ero! cùm, fine duelli,
  Clauserit extremas pugna peracta vices,
Tum tibi, si placeat, fugientia tempora reddam;
  Sufficiet votis ista iuuenta meis.

III. Ad eundem

In Monstrum vocabuli Anti-Tami-Cami-
Categoria

O QVAM bellus homo es! lepido quàm nomine fingis
  Istas *Anti-Tami-Cami-Categorias!*
Sic Catharis noua sola placent; res, verba nouantur:
  Quae sapiunt aeuum, ceu cariosa iacent.
Quin liceat nobis aliquas procudere voces:
  Non tibi fingendi sola taberna patet.
Cùm sacra perturbet vester furor omnia, scriptum
  Hoc erit, *Anti-furi-Puri-Categoria.*
Pollubra vel cùm olim damnâris Regiâ in arâ,
  Est *Anti-pelvi-Melvi-Categoria.*

IV. *Partitio* Anti-Tami-Cami-Categoriae

TRES video partes, quò re distinctiùs vtar,
  Anticategoriae, Scoto-Britanne, tuae:

Ritibus vna Sacris opponitur; altera Sanctos
  Praedicat autores; tertia plena Deo est.
Postremis ambabus idem sentimus vterque;
  Ipse pios laudo; Numen & ipse colo.
Non nisi prima suas patiuntur praelia lites.
  O bene quòd dubium possideamus agrum!

v. *In metri genus*

CVR, vbi tot ludat numeris antiqua poesis,
  Sola tibi Sappho, femináque vna placet?
Cur tibi tam facilè non arrisêre poetae
  Heroum grandi carmina fulta pede?
Cur non lugentes Elegi? non acer Iambus?
  Commotos animos rectiùs ista decent.
Scilicet hoc vobis proprium, qui puriùs itis,
  Et populi spurcas creditis esse vias:
Vos ducibus missis, missis doctoribus, omnes
  Femineum blandâ fallitis arte genus:
Nunc etiam teneras quò versus gratior aures
  Mulceat, imbelles complacuêre modi.

vi. *De Laruatâ Gorgone*

GORGONA cur diram laruásque obtrudis inanes,
  Cùm propè sit nobis Musa, Medusa procul?
Si, quia felices olim dixêre poetae
  Pallada gorgoneam, sic tua verba placent.
Vel potiùs liceat distinguere. Túque tuíque
  Sumite *gorgoneam*, nostráque *Pallas* erit.

VII. *De Praesulum fastu*

PRAESVLIBVS nostris fastus, *Melvine*, tumentes
    Saepiùs aspergis. Siste, pudore vacas.
An quod semotum populo laquearibus altis
    Eminet, id tumidum protinus esse feres?
Ergo etiam Solem dicas, ignaue, superbum,
    Qui tam sublimi conspicit orbe viam:
Ille tamen, quamuis altus, tua crimina ridens
    Assiduo vilem lumine cingit humum.
Sic laudandus erit nactus sublimia Praesul,
    Qui dulci miseros irradiabit ope.

VIII. *De geminâ Academiâ*

QVIS hìc superbit, oro? túne, an Praesules,
    Quos dente nigro corripis?
Tu duplicem solus Camoenarum thronum
    Virtute percellis tuâ;
Et vnus impar aestimatur viribus,
    Vtrumque sternis calcitro:
Omnésque stulti audimus, aut hypocritae,
    Te perspicaci atque integro.
An rectiùs nos, si vices vertas, probi,
    Te contumaci & liuido?
Quisquis tuetur perspicillis Belgicis
    Quâ parte tractari solent,
Res ampliantur, sin per aduersam videt,
    Minora fiunt omnia:
Tu qui superbos caeteros existimas
    (Superbius cùm te nihil)
Vertas specillum: nam, prout se res habent,
    Vitro minùs rectè vteris.

IX. *De S. Baptismi Ritu*

Cvm tener ad sacros infans sistatur aquales,
  Quòd puer ignorat, verba profana putas?
Annon sic mercamur agros? quibus ecce Redemptor
  Comparat aeterni regna beata Dei.
Scilicet emptorem si res aut parcior aetas
  Impediant, apices legis amicus obit.
Forsitan & prohibes infans portetur ad vndas,
  Et per se Templi limen adire velis:
Sin, *Melvine*, pedes alienos postulet infans,
  Cur sic displiceat vox aliena tibi?
Rectiùs innocuis lactentibus omnia praestes,
  Quae ratio per se, si sit adulta, facit.
Quid vetat vt pueri vagitus suppleat alter,
  Cùm nequeat claras ipse litare preces?
Saeuus es eripiens paruis vadimonia coeli:
  Et tibi sit nemo praes, vbi poscis opem.

X. *De Signaculo Crucis*

Cvr tanta sufflas probra in innocuam Crucem?
Non plùs maligni daemones Christi cruce
Vnquam fugari, quàm tui socij solent.
Apostolorum culpa non leuis fuit
Vitâsse Christi spiritum efflantis crucem.
Et Christianus quisque piscis dicitur
Tertulliano, propter vndae pollubrum,
Quo tingimur parui. Ecquis autem brachijs
Natare sine clarissimâ potest cruce?
Sed non moramur: namque vestra crux erit,
Vobis fauentibúsue, vel negantibus.

XI. *De iuramento Ecclesiae*

ARTICVLIS sacris quidam subscribere iussus,
 Ah! Cheiragra vetat, quò minùs, inquit, agam.
O veré dictum, & bellè! cùm torqueat omnes
 Ordinis osores articulare malum.

XII. *De Purificatione post puerperium*

ENIXAS pueros matres se sistere templis
 Displicet, & laudis tura litare Deo.
Fortè quidem, cùm per vestras Ecclesia turbas
 Fluctibus internis exagitata natet,
Vos sine maternis hymnis infantia vidit,
 Vitáque neglectas est saùs vlta preces.
Sed nos, cùm nequeat paruorum lingua, parentem
 Non laudare Deum, credimus esse nefas.
Quotidiana suas poscant si fercula grates,
 Nostra caro sanctae nescia laudis erit?

Adde pijs animis quaeuis occasio lucro est,
 Quâ possint humili fundere corde preces.
Sic vbi iam mulier decerpti conscia pomi
 Ingemat ob partus, ceu maledicta, suos,
Appositè quem commotum subfugerat olim,
 Nunc redit ad mitem, ceu benedicta, Deum.

XIII. *De Antichristi decore Pontificali*

NON quia Pontificum sunt olim afflata veneno,
 Omnia sunt temere proijcienda foras.
Tollantur si cuncta malus quae polluit vsus,
 Non remanent nobis corpora, non animae.

XIV. *De Superpelliceo*

QVID sacrae tandem meruêre vestes,
Quas malus liuor iaculis lacessit
Polluens castum chlamydis colorem
      Dentibus atris?

Quicquid ex vrnâ meliore ductum
Luce praelustri, vel honore pollet,
Mens sub insigni specie coloris
      Concipit albi.

Scilicet talem liquet esse solem;
Angeli vultu radiante candent;
Incolae coeli melioris albâ
      Veste triumphant.

E creaturis sine mentis vsu
Conditis binas homini sequendas
Spiritus proponit, & est vtrique
      Candor amicus.

Ergo ringantur pietatis hostes,
Filij noctis, populus malignus,
Dum suum nomen tenet, & triumphat
      Albion albo.

XV. *De Pileo quadrato*

QVAE dicteria fuderat Britannus
Superpellicei tremendus hostis,
Isthaec pileus audijt propinquus,
Et partem capitis petit supremam;
Non sic effugit angulus vel vnus
Quò dictis minùs acribus notetur.

Verùm heus! si reputes, tibi tuísque
Longè pileus anteit galerum,
Vt feruor cerebri refrigeretur,
Qui vestras edit intimè medullas.
Sed qui tam malè pileos habetis,
Quos Ecclesia comprobat, verendum
Ne tandem caput eius impetatis.

XVI. *In Catharum*

CVR Latiam linguam reris nimis esse profanam,
  Quam praemissa probant secula, nostra probant?
Cur teretem Graecam damnas, atque Hellada totam,
  Quâ tamen occisi foedera scripta Dei?
Scilicet Hebraeam cantas, & perstrepis vnam:
  Haec facit ad nasum sola loquela tuum.

XVII. *De Episcopis*

QVOS charos habuit Christus Apostolos,
Testatósque suo tradiderat gregi;
Vt, cùm mors rabidis vnguibus imminens
Doctrinae fluuios clauderet aureae,
Mites acciperent Lampada Praesules,
Seruaréntque sacrum clauibus ordinem;
Hos nunc barbaries impia vellicat
Indulgens proprijs ambitionibus,
Et, quos ipsa nequit scandere vertices,
Hos ad se trahere et mergere gestiens.
O caecum populum! si bona res siet
Praesul, cur renuis? sin mala, pauculos
Quàm cunctos fieri praestat Episcopos.

XVIII. Ad Melvinum

De ijsdem

PRAESVLIBVS dirum te Musa coarguit hostem,
  An quia Textores Artificésque probas?

XIX. De Textore Catharo

CVM piscatores Textor legit esse vocatos,
  Vt sanctum Domini persequerentur opus;
Ille quoque inuadit Diuinam Flaminis artem,
  Subtegmen reti dignius esse putans,
Et nunc perlongas Scripturae stamine telas
  Torquet, & in Textu Doctor vtroque cluet.

XX. De Magicis rotatibus

QVOS tu rotatus, quale murmur auscultas
In ritibus nostris? Ego audio nullum.
Agè, prouocemus vsque ad Angelos ipsos,
Auuésque superas: arbitri ipsi sint litis,
Vtrum tenore sacra nostra sint nécne
Aequabili facta. Ecquid ergo te tanta
Calumniandi concitauit vrtica,
Vt, quae Papicolis propria, assuas nobis,
Falsúmque potiùs quàm crepes (verum) versu?
Tu perstrepis tamen; vtque turgeat carmen
Tuum tibi, poeta belle, non mystes,
Magicos rotatus, & perhorridas Striges,
Dicterijs mordacibus notans, clamas
Non conuenire precibus ista Diuinis.
O saeuus hostis! quàm ferociter pugnas!
Nihílne respondebimus tibi? Fatemur.

XXI. *Ad fratres*

O SEC'LVM lepidum! circumstant vndique Fratres,
  Papicolísque sui sunt, Catharísque sui.
Sic nunc plena boni sunt omnia Fratris, amore
  Cùm nil fraterno rarius esse queat.

XXII. *De labe maculísque*

LABECVLAS maculásque nobis obijcis:
Quid? hoccine est mirum? Viatores sumus.
Quò sanguis est Christi, nisi vt maculas lauet,
Quas spargit animae corporis propius lutum?
Vos ergo puri! o nomen appositissimum
Quo vulgus ornat vos! At audias parum;
Astronomus olim (vt fama) dum maculas diu,
Quas Luna habet, tuetur, in foueam cadit,
Totúsque caenum Cynthiae ignoscit notis.
Ecclesia est mihi Luna; perge in Fabulâ.

XXIII. *De Musicâ Sacrâ*

CVR efficaci, Deucalion, manu,
Post restitutos fluctibus obices,
  Mutas in humanam figuram
    Saxa superuacuásque cautes?

Quin redde formas, o bone, pristinas,
Et nos reducas ad lapides auos:
  Nam saxa mirantur canentes,
    Saxa lyras citharásque callent.

Rupes tenaces & silices ferunt
Potentióri carmine percitas
  Saltus per incultos lacúsque
    Orphea mellifluum secutas.

Et saxa diris hispida montibus
Amphionis testudine nobili
   Percussa dum currunt ad vrbem
    Moenia contribuêre Thebis.

Tantùm repertum est trux hominum genus,
Qui templa sacris expoliant choris,
   Non erubescentes vel ipsas
    Duritiâ superare cautes.

O plena centum Musica Gratijs,
Praeclariorum spirituum cibus,
   Quò me vocas tandem, tuúmque
    Vt celebrem decus insusurras?

Tu Diua miro pollice spiritum
Caeno profani corporis exuens
   Ter millies coelo reponis:
    Astra rogant, Nouus hic quis hospes?

Ardore Moses concitus entheo,
Mersis reuertens laetus ab hostibus
   Exuscitat plebem sacratos
    Ad Dominum properare cantus.

Quid hocce? Psalmos audión'? o dapes!
O succulenti balsama spiritûs!
   Ramenta coeli, guttulaéque
    Deciduae melioris orbis!

Quos David, ipsae deliciae Dei,
Ingens piorum gloria Principum,
   Sionis excelsas ad arces
    Cum citharis lituísque miscet.

Miratur aequor finitimum sonos,
Et ipse Iordan sistit aquas stupens;
   Prae quo Tibris vultum recondit,
      Eridanúsque pudore fusus.

Tún' obdis aures, grex noue, barbaras,
Et nullus audis? cantibus obstrepens,
   Vt, quò fatiges verberésque
      Pulpita, plus spatij lucreris?

At cui videri prodigium potest
Mentes, quietis tympana publicae,
   Discordijs plenas sonoris
      Harmoniam tolerare nullam?

XXIV. *De câdem*

CANTVS sacros, profane, mugitus vocas?
Mugire multò mauelim quàm rudere.

XXV. *De rituum vsu*

CVM primùm ratibus suis
nostram Caesar ad insulam
olim appelleret, intuens
omnes indigenas loci
viuentes sine vestibus,
O victoria, clamitat,
certa, ac perfacilis mihi!
   Non alio Cathari modo
dum sponsam Domini pijs
orbam ritibus expetunt,
atque ad barbariem patrum
vellent omnia regredi,
illam tegminis insciam

prorsus Daemoni & hostibus
exponunt superabilem.
    Atqui vos secus, o boni,
sentire ac sapere addecet,
si vestros animos regant
Scripturae canones sacrae:
Namque haec, iure, cuipiam
vestem non adimi suam,
sed nudis & egentibus
non suam tribui iubet.

XXVI. *De annulo coniugali*

SED nec coniugij signum, Melvine, probabis?
   Nec vel tantillum pignus habebit amor?
Nulla tibi si signa placent, è nubibus arcum
   Eripe coelesti qui moderatur aquae.
Illa quidem à nostro non multùm abludit imago,
   Annulus & plenus tempore forsan erit.
Sin nebulis parcas, & nostro parcito signo,
   Cui non absimilis sensus inesse solet.
Scilicet, vt quos ante suas cum coniuge tedas
   Merserat in lustris perniciosa venus,
Annulus hos reuocet, sistátque libidinis vndas
   Legitimi signum connubiale tori.

XXVII. *De Mundis & mundanis*

Ex praelio vndae ignísque (si Physicis fides)
      Tranquillus aer nascitur:
Sic ex profano Cosmico & Catharo potest
      Christianus extundi bonus.

XXVIII. *De oratione Dominicâ*

QVAM Christus immortalis innocuo gregi
    voce suâ dederat,
        quis crederet mortalibus
orationem reijci septemplicem,
    quae miseris clypeo
        Aiacis est praestantior?
Haec verba superos aduolaturus thronos
    Christus, vt auxilij
        nos haud inanes linqueret,
(cùm dignius nil posset aut melius dare)
    pignora chara sui
        fruenda nobis tradidit.
Quis sic amicum excipiet, vt Cathari Deum,
    qui renouare sacri
        audent amoris Symbolum?
Tu verò quisquis es, caue ne, dum neges,
    improbe, verba Dei,
        te deneget VERBVM Deus.

XXIX. *In Catharum quendam*

CVM templis effare, madent sudaria, mappae,
    Trux caper alarum, suppara, laena, sagum.
Quin populo, clemens, aliquid largire caloris:
    Nunc sudas solus; caetera turba riget.

XXX. *De lupâ lustri Vaticani*

CALVMNIARVM nec pudor quis nec modus?
Nec *Vaticanae* desines vnquam *Lupae*
Metus inanes? Nos pari praeteruehi

Illam Charybdim cautione nouimus
Vestrámque Scyllam, aequis parati spiculis
Britannicam in Vulpem, ínque Romanam Lupam.
Dicti fidem firmabimus Anagrammate.

XXXI. *De impositione manuum*

NEC dextra te fugit, almi Amoris emblema?
Atqui manus imponere integras praestat,
Quàm (more vestro) imponere inscio vulgo.
Quantò Impositio melior est Imposturâ!

XXXII. *Supplicum Ministrorum raptus*
κωμῳδούμενος

　　AMBITIO Cathari quinque constat Actibus.
　I. Primò, vnus aut alter parum ritus placet:
　　　Iam repit impietas volatura illico.
　II. Mox displicent omnes. Vbi hoc permanserit
III. Paulò, secretis mussitans in angulis
　　　Quaerit recessus. Incalescit fabula:
IV. Erumpit inde, & contineri nescius
　V. Syluas pererrat. Fibulis dein omnibus
　　　Prae spiritu ruptis, quò eas resarciat
　　　Amstellodamum corripit se. *Plaudite.*

XXXIII. *De Autorum enumeratione*

Qvò magis inuidiam nobis & crimina confles,
　Pertrahis in partes nomina magna tuas;
Martyra, Calvinum, Bezam, doctúmque *Bucerum,*
　Qui tamen in nostros fortiter ire negant.
Whitaker, erranti quem praefers carmine, miles
　Assiduus nostri papilionis erat.

Nos quoque possemus longas conscribere turmas,
 Si numero starent praelia, non animis.
Primus adest nobis, Pharisaeis omnibus hostis,
 Christus Apostolici cinctus amore gregis.
Tu geminas belli portas, o *Petre*, repandis,
 Dum gladium stringens *Paulus* ad arma vocat.
Inde Patres pergunt quadrati, & tota Vetustas.
 Nempe Nouatores quis Veteranus amat?
Iam *Constantinus* multo se milite miscet;
 Inuisámque tuis erigit hasta Crucem.
Hipponensis adest properans, & torquet in hostes
 Lampada, quâ studijs inuigilare solet.
Téque Deum alternis cantans *Ambrosius* iram,
 Immemor antiqui mellis, eundo coquit.
Haec etiam ad pugnam praesens, quâ viuimus, aetas
 Innumeram nostris partibus addit opem.
Quos inter plenúsque Deo genióque Iacobus
 Defendit veram mente manúque *fidem*.
Interea ad sacrum stimulat sacra Musica bellum,
 Quâ sine vos miseri lentiùs itis ope.
Militat & nobis, quem vos contemnitis, Ordo;
 Ordine discerni maxima bella solent.
O vos inualidos! Audi quem talibus armis
 Euentum Naso vidit et admonuit;
Vna dies Catharos ad bellum miserat omnes:
 Ad bellum missos perdidit vna dies.

XXXIV. *De auri sacrâ fame*

CLAVDIS auaritiâ Satyram; statuísque sacrorum
 Esse recidendas, Aeace noster, opes.
Caetera condonabo tibi, scombrísque remittam:
 Sacrilegum carmen, censeo, flamma voret.

XXXV. *Ad Scotiam. Protrepticon ad Pacem*

SCOTIA quae frigente iaces porrecta sub Arcto,
   Cur adeò immodicâ relligione cales?
Anne tuas flammas ipsa Antiperistasis auget,
   Vt niue torpentes incaluêre manus?
Aut vt pruna gelu summo mordaciùs vrit,
   Sic acuunt zelum frigora tanta tuum?
Quin nocuas extingue faces, precor: vnda propinqua es
   Et tibi vicinas porrigit aequor aquas:
Aut potiùs Christi sanguis demissus ab alto,
   Vicinúsque magìs nobiliórque fluit:
Ne, si flamma nouis adolescat mota flabellis,
   Ante diem vestro mundus ab igne ruat.

XXXVI. *Ad seductos innocentes*

INNOCVAE mentes, quibus inter flumina mundi
   Ducitur illimi candida vita fide,
Absit vt ingenuum pungant mea verba pudorem;
   Perstringunt vestros carmina sola duces.
O vtinam aut illorum oculi (quod comprecor vnum)
   Vobis, aut illis pectora vestra forent.

XXXVII. *Ad Melvinum*

ATQVI te precor vnicè per ipsam,
Quae scripsit numeros, manum; per omnes
Musarum calices, per & beatos
Sarcasmos quibus artifex triumphas;
Quin per Presbyteros tuos; per vrbem
Quam curto nequeo referre versu;
Per charas tibi nobilésque dextras,

Quas subscriptio neutiquam inquinauit;
Per quicquid tibi suauiter probatur;
Ne me carminibus nimis dicacem,
Aut saeuum reputes. Amica nostra est
Atque edentula Musa, nec veneno
Splenis perlita contumeliosi.

Nam si te cuperem secare versu,
Totámque euomerem potenter iram
Quam aut Ecclesia despicata vobis,
Aut laesae mihi suggerunt Athenae,
(Et quem non stimularet haec simultas?)
Iam te funditus igneis Camoenis,
Et Musâ crepitante subruissem:
Omnis linea sepiam recusans
Plumbo ducta fuisset aestuanti,
Centum stigmatibus tuos inurens
Profanos fremitus bonásque sannas:
Plùs charta haec mea delibuta dictis
Haesisset tibi, quàm suprema vestis
Olim accreuerit *Herculi* furenti:
Quin hoc carmine Lexicon probrorum
Extruxissem, vbi, cùm moneret vsus,
Haurirent tibi tota plaustra Musae.

Nunc haec omnia sustuli, tonantes
Affectus socijs tuis remittens.
Non te carmine turbidum vocaui,
Non deridiculúmue, siue ineptum,
Non striges, magiámue, vel rotatus,
Non fastus tibi turgidos repono;
Errores, maculas, superbiámque,
Labes, somniáque, ambitúsque diros,
Tinnitus *Berecynthios* omittens
Nil horum regero tibi merenti.

Quin te laudibus orno: quippe dico,
Caesar sobrius ad rei Latinae

Vnus dicitur aduenire cladem:
Et tu solus ad *Angliae* procellas
(Cùm plerumque tuâ sodalitate
Nil sit crassius, impolitiúsue)
Accedis bene doctus, et poeta.

XXXVIII. *Ad Eundem*

INCIPIS irridens; stomachans in carmine pergis;
Desinis exclamans: tota figura, vale.

XXXIX. *Ad Seren. Regem*

ECCE pererratas, Regum doctissime, nugas,
Quas gens inconsulta, suis vexata procellis,
Libandas nobis absorbendásque propinat!
O caecos animi fratres! quis vestra fatigat
Corda furor, spissâque afflat caligine sensus?
Cernite, quàm formosa suas Ecclesia pennas
Explicat, & radijs ipsum pertingit Olympum!
Vicini populi passim mirantur, & aequos
Mentibus attonitis cupiunt addiscere ritus:
Angelicae turmae nostris se coetibus addunt:
Ipse etiam Christus coelo speculatus ab alto,
Intuitúque vno stringens habitacula mundi,
Sola mihi plenos, ait, exhibet *Anglia* cultus.
Scilicet has olim diuisas aequore terras
Seposuit Diuina sibi, cùm conderet orbem,
Progenies, gemmámque suâ quasi pyxide clausit.

    O qui *Defensor Fidei* meritissimus audis,
Responde aeternùm titulo; quóque ordine felix
Coepisti, pergas simili res texere filo.

Obrue feruentes, ruptis conatibus, hostes:
Quásque habet aut patulas, aut caeco tramite, moles
Haeresis, euertas. Quid enim te fallere possit?
Tu venas laticésque omnes, quos sacra recludit
Pagina, gustâsti, multóque interprete gaudes:
Tu Synodósque, Patrésque, & quod dedit alta vetustas
Haud per te moritura, Scholámque introspicis omnem.
Nec transire licet quo mentis acumine findis
Viscera naturae, commistúsque omnibus astris
Ante tuum tempus coelum gratissimus ambis.
Hâc ope munitus securior excipis vndas,
Quas Latij Catharíque mouent, atque inter vtrasque
Pastor agis proprios, medio tutissimus, agnos.

    Perge, decus Regum; sic, Augustissime, plures
Sint tibi vel stellis laudes, & laudibus anni:
Sic pulsare tuas, exclusis luctibus, ausint
Gaudia sola fores: sic quicquid somnia mentis
Intus agunt, habeat certum meditatio finem:
Sic positis nugis, quibus irretita libido
Innumeros mergit vitiatâ mente poetas,
Sola *Iacobaeum* decantent carmina nomen.

XL. *Ad Deum*

QVEM tu, summe Deus, semel
Scribentem placido rore beaueris,
    Illum non labor irritus
Exercet miserum; non dolor vnguium
    Morsus increpat anxios;
Non maeret calamus; non queritur caput:
    Sed faecunda poëseωs
Vis, & vena sacris regnat in artubus;
    Qualis nescius aggerum
Exundat fluuio Nilus amabili.

O dulcissime Spiritus,
Sanctos qui gemitus mentibus inseris
A Te Turture defluos,
Quòd scribo, & placeo, si placeo, tuum est.

FINIS

PASSIO DISCERPTA

I. *Ad Dominum morientem*

Cvm lacrymas oculósque duos tot vulnera vincant,
   Impar, & in fletum vel resolutus, ero;
Sepia concurrat, peccatis aptior humor,
   Et mea iam lacrymet culpa colore suo.

II. *In sudorem sanguineum*

Qvò fugies, sudor? quamuìs pars altera Christi
   Nescia sit metae; venula, cella tua est.
Si tibi non illud placeat mirabile corpus,
   Caetera displiceat turba, necesse, tibi:
Ni me fortè petas; nam quantò indignior ipse,
   Tu mihi subueniens dignior esse potes.

III. *In eundem*

Sic tuus effundi gestit pro crimine sanguis,
   Vt nequeat paulò se cohibere domi.

IV. *In latus perfossum*

Christe, vbi tam duro patet in te semita ferro,
   Spero meo cordi posse patere viam.

v. *In Sputum & Conuicia*

O BARBAROS! sic os rependitis sanctum,
  Visum quod vni praebet, omnibus vitam,
  Sputando, praedicando? sic Aquas vitae
  Contaminatis alueósque caelestes
  Sputando, blasphemando? nempe ne hoc fiat
  In posterum, maledicta Ficus arescens
  Gens tota fiet, atque vtrinque plectetur.
  Parate situlas, Ethnici, lagenásque,
  Graues lagenas, Vester est Aquae ductus.

vi. *In Coronam spineam*

CHRISTE, dolor tibi supplicio, mihi blanda voluptas;
  Tu spinâ miserè pungeris, ipse Rosâ.
Spicula mutemus: capias Tu serta Rosarum,
  Qui Caput es, spinas & tua Membra tuas.

vii. *In Arund. Spin. Genuflex. Purpur.*

QVÀM nihil illudis, Gens improba! quàm malè cedunt
  Scommata! Pastorem semper Arundo decet.
Quàm nihil illudis! cùm quò magìs angar acuto
  Munere, Rex tantò verior inde prober.
Quàm nihil illudis flectens! namque integra posthâc
  Posteritas flectet córque genúque mihi.
Quàm nihil illudis! si, quae tua purpura fingit,
  Purpureo meliùs sanguine Regna probem.
At non lusus erit, si quem tu laeta necasti
  Viuat, & in mortem vita sit illa tuam.

VIII. *In Alapas*

AH! quàm caederis hinc & inde palmis!
Sic vnguenta solent manu fricari:
Sic toti medicaris ipse mundo.

IX. *In Flagellum*

CHRISTE, flagellati spes & victoria mundi,
  Crimina cùm turgent, & mea poena prope est,
Suauiter admoueas notum tibi carne flagellum,
  Sufficiat virgae saepiùs vmbra tuae.
Mitis agas: tenerae duplicant sibi verbera mentes,
  Ipsáque sunt ferulae mollia corda suae.

X. *In vestes diuisas*

SI, Christe, dum suffigeris, tuae vestes
  Sunt hostium legata, non amicorum,
Vt postulat mos; quid tuis dabis? Teipsum.

XI. *In pium Latronem*

O NIMIVM Latro! reliquis furatus abundè,
  Nunc etiam Christum callidus aggrederis.

XII. *In Christum crucem ascensurum*

ZACCHAEVS, vt Te cernat, arborem scandit:
Nunc ipse scandis, vt labore mutato
Nobis facilitas cedat & tibi sudor.
Sic omnibus videris ad modum visûs.
Fides gigantem sola, vel facit nanum.

XIII. *Christus in cruce*

HIC, vbi sanati stillant opobalsama mundi,
  Aduoluor madidae laetus hiánsque Cruci:
Pro lapsu stillarum abeunt peccata; nec acres
  Sanguinis insultus exanimata ferunt.
Christe, fluas semper; ne, si tua flumina cessent,
  Culpa redux iugem te neget esse Deum.

XIV. *In Clauos*

QVALIS eras, qui, ne melior natura minorem
  Eriperet nobis, in Cruce fixus eras;
Iam meus es: nunc Te teneo: Pastórque prehensus
  Hoc ligno, his clauis est, quasi Falce suâ.

XV. *Inclinato capite.* Joh. 19

VVLPIBVS antra feris, nidíque volucribus adsunt,
  Quodque suum nouit strôma, cubile suum.
Qui tamen excipiat, Christus caret hospite: tantùm
  In cruce suspendens, vnde reclinet, habet.

XVI. *Ad Solem deficientem*

QVID hoc? & ipse deficis, Caeli gigas,
  Almi choragus luminis?
Tu promis Orbem manè, condis vesperi,
  Mundi fidelis clauiger:
At nunc fatiscis. Nempe Dominus aedium
  Prodegit integrum penu,

Quámque ipse lucis tesseram sibi negat,
    Negat familiae suae.
Carere discat verna, quo summus caret
    Paterfamilias lumine.
Tu verò mentem neutiquam despondeas,
    Resurget occumbens Herus:
Tunc instruetur lautiùs radijs penu,
    Tibi supererunt & mihi.

XVII. *Monumenta aperta*

Dvm moreris, Mea Vita, ipsi vixere sepulti,
    Próque vno vincto turba soluta fuit.
Tu tamen, haud tibi tam moreris, quàm viuis in illis,
    Asserit & vitam Mors animata tuam.
Scilicet in tumulis Crucifixum quaerite, viuit:
    Conuincunt vnam multa sepulcra Crucem.
Sic, pro Maiestate, Deum, non perdere vitam
    Quam tribuit, verùm multiplicare decet.

XVIII. *Terrae-motus*

Te fixo vel Terra mouet: nam, cum Cruce, totam
    Circumferre potes; Sampson vt antè fores.
Heu stolidi, primùm fugientem figite Terram,
    Tunc Dominus clauis aggrediendus erit.

XIX. *Velum scissum*

Frvstra, Verpe, tumes, propola cultûs,
    Et Templi parasite; namque velum
Diffissum reserat Deum latentem,

Et pomoeria terminósque sanctos
Non vrbem facit vnicam, sed Orbem.
Et pro pectoribus recenset aras,
Dum cor omne suum sibi requirat
Structorem, & Solomon vbique regnet.
Nunc Arcana patent, nec inuolutam
Phylacteria complicant latrîam.
Excessit tener Orbis ex Ephebis,
Maturúsque suos coquens amores
Praeflorat sibi nuptias futuras.
Vbique est Deus, Agnus, Ara, Flamen.

xx. *Petrae scissae*

SANVS Homo factus, vitiorum purus vterque;
   At sibi collisit fictile Daemon opus.
Post vbi Mosaicae repararent fragmina Leges,
   Infectas tabulas facta iuuenca scidit.
Haud aliter cùm Christus obit, prae funere tanto
   Constat inaccessas dissiluisse petras.
Omnia, praeter corda, scelus confregit & error,
   Quae contrita tamen caetera damna leuant.

xxi. *In Mundi sympathiam cum Christo*

NON moreris solus: Mundus simul interit in te,
   Agnoscítque tuam Machina tota Crucem.
Hunc ponas animam mundi, Plato: vel tua mundum
   Ne nimium vexet quaestio, pone meam.

LVCVS

I. *Homo, Statua*

SVM, quis nescit, Imago Dei, sed saxea certè:
  Hanc mihi duritiem contulit improbitas.
Durescunt proprijs euulsa corallia fundis,
  Haud secus ingenitis dotibus orbus Adam.
Tu, qui cuncta creans docuisti marmora flere,
  Haud mihi cor saxo durius esse sinas.

II. *Patria*

VT tenuis flammae species caelum vsque minatur,
  Igniculos legans, manserit ipsa licet;
Sic mucronatam reddunt suspiria mentem,
  Votáque scintillae sunt animosa meae.
Assiduo stimulo carnem Mens vlta lacessit,
  Sedula si fuerit, perterebrare potest.

III. *In Stephanum lapidatum*

QVI silicem tundit, (mirum tamen) elicit ignem:
  At Caelum è saxis elicuit Stephanus.

IV. *In Simonem Magum*

ECQVID emes Christum? pro nobis scilicet olim
  Venditus est Agnus, non tamen emptus erit.
Quin nos Ipse emit, precioso faenora soluens
  Sanguine: nec precium merx emit vlla suum.

243

Ecquid emes Caelum? quin stellam rectiùs vnam
   Quo precio venit, fac, liceare priùs.
Nempe graui fertur scelerata pecunia motu,
   Si sursum iacias, in caput ipsa ruit.
Vnicus est nummus, caelo Christóque petitus,
   Nempe in quo clarè lucet Imago Dei.

v. *In S. Scripturas*

HEV, quis spiritus, igneúsque turbo
Regnat visceribus, meásque versat
Imo pectore cogitationes?
Nunquid pro foribus sedendo nuper
Stellam vespere suxerim volantem,
Haec autem hospitio latere turpi
Prorsùs nescia, cogitat recessum?
Nunquid mel comedens, apem comedi
Ipsâ cum dominâ domum vorando?
Imò, me nec apes, nec astra pungunt:
Sacratissima Charta, tu fuisti
Quae cordis latebras sinúsque caecos
Atque omnes peragrata es angiportus
Et flexus fugientis appetitûs.
Ah, quàm docta perambulare calles
Maeandrósque plicásque, quàm perita es!
Quae vis condidit, ipsa nouit aedes.

VI. *In pacem Britannicam*

ANGLIA cur solùm fuso sine sanguine sicca est,
   Cùm natet in tantis caetera terra malis?
Sit licet in pelago semper, sine fluctibus illa est,
   Cùm qui plus terrae, plus habuere maris.

Naufragij causa est alijs mare, roboris Anglo,
    Et quae corrumpit moenia, murus aqua est.
Nempe hìc Religio floret, regina quietis,
    Túque super nostras, Christe, moueris aquas.

VII. *Auaritia*

A V R V M nocte videns, vidisse insomnia dicit:
    Aurum luce videns, nulla videre putat.
O falsos homines! Vigilat, qui somniat aurum,
    Plúsque habet hic laetus, quàm vel Auarus habet.

VIII. *In Lotionem pedum Apostolorum*

S O L E M ex Occano Veteres exurgere fingunt
    Postquam se gelidis nocte refecit aquis:
Veriùs hoc olim factum est, vbi, Christe, lauares
    Illos, qui mundum circumiere, pedes.

IX. *In D. Lucam*

C V R Deus elegit Medicum, qui numine plenus
    Diuinâ Christi scriberet acta manu?
Vt discat sibi quisque, quid vtile: nempe nocebat
    Crudum olim pomum, tristis Adame, tibi.

X. Papae titulus

Nec Deus Nec Homo

Q V I S N A M Antichristus cessemus quaerere; Papa
Nec Deus est nec Homo: Christus vterque fuit.

XI. *Tributi solutio*

PISCIS tributum soluit; & tu Caesari:
Vtrumque mirum est: hoc tamen mirum magìs,
Quòd omnibus tute imperes, nemo tibi.

XII. *Tempestas Christo dormiente*

CVM dormis, surgit pelagus: cùm, Christe, resurgis,
Dormitat pelagus: Quàm bene fraena tenes!

XIII. *Bonus Ciuis*

SAGAX Humilitas, eligens viros bonos
Atque euehens, bonum facit faecundius,
Quàm si ipse solus omnia interuerteret,
Suámque in alijs possidet prudentiam.

XIV. *In Vmbram Petri*

PRODVXIT Vmbram corpus, Vmbra corpori
Vitam reduxit: ecce gratitudinem.

XV. *Martha: Maria*

CHRISTVS adest: crebris aedes percurrite scopis,
Excutite aulaea, & luceat igne focus.
Omnia purgentur, niteat mihi tota supellex,
Parcite luminibus, sítque lucerna domus:
O cessatrices! eccum puluisculus illìc!
Corde tuo forsan, caetera munda, SOROR.

XVI. *Amor*

QVID metuant homines infrà, supráue minentur
  Sydera, pendenti sedulus aure bibis:
Vtque ouis in dumis, haeres in crine Cometae,
  Sollicitus, ne te stella perita notet:
Omnia quaerendo, sed te, super omnia, vexas:
  Et quid tu tandem desidiosus? AMO.

XVII. *In Superbum*

MAGNAS es; esto. Bulla si vocaberis,
Largiar & istud: scilicet Magnatibus
Difficilis esse haud soleo: nam, pol, si forem,
Ipsi sibi sunt nequiter facillimi.
Quin, mitte nugas; téque carnem & sanguinem
Communem habere crede cum Cerdonibus:
Illum volo, qui calceat lixam tuum.

XVIII. *In eundem*

VNVSQVISQVE hominum, Terra est; & filius arui.
  Dic mihi, mons sterilis, vallis an vber eris?

XIX. *Afflictio*

QVOS tu calcasti fluctus, me, Christe, lacessunt,
  Transiliúntque caput, qui subiere pedes.
Christe, super fluctus si non discurrere detur:
  Per fluctus saltem, fac, precor, ipse vadem.

XX. *In κενοδοξίαν*

QVI sugit auido spiritu rumusculos
Et flatulentas aucupatur glorias,
Foelicitatis culmen extra se locat,
Spargítque per tot capita, quot vulgus gerit.
Tu verò collige te, tibíque insistito,
Breuiore nodo stringe vitae sarcinas,
Rotundus in te: namque si ansatus sies,
Te mille rixae, mille prensabunt doli,
Ducéntque, donec incidentem in cassidem
Te mille nasi, mille rideant sinus.
Quare, peritus nauta, vela contrahas,
Famámque nec difflaueris, nec suxeris:
Tuásque librans actiones, gloriam
Si ducat agmen, reprime; sin claudat, sinas.
Morosus, oxygala est: leuis, coagulum.

XXI. *In Gulosum*

DVM prono rapis ore cibos, & fercula verris,
   Intra extráque graui plenus es illuuie.
Non iam ventriculus, verùm spelunca vocetur
   Illa cauerna, in quâ tot coiere ferae.
Ipse fruare, licet, solus graueolente sepulcro;
   Te petet, ante diem quisquis obire cupit.

XXII. *In Improbum disertum*

SERICVS es dictis, factis pannusia Baucis:
   Os & lingua tibi diues, egena manus:
Ni facias, vt opes linguae per brachia serpant,
   Aurea pro naulo lingua Charontis erit.

XXIII. *Consolatio*

CVR lacrymas & tarda trahis suspiria, tanquam
  Nunc primùm socij mors foret atra tui?
Nos autem, à cunis, omnes sententia Mortis
  Quotidie iugulat, nec semel vllus obit.
Viuimus in praesens: hesternam viuere vitam
  Nemo potest: hodie vita sepulta prior.
Trecentos obijt Nestor, non transijt annos,
  Vel quia tot moritur, tot viguisse probes.
Dum lacrymas, it vita: tuus tibi clepsydra fletus,
  Et numerat mortes singula gutta pares;
Frustra itaque in tot funeribus miraberis vnum,
  Sera nimis lacryma haec, si lacrymabis, erit.
Siste tuum fletum & gemitus: namque imbribus istis
  Ac zephyris, carnis flos remeare nequit.
Nec tu pro socio doleas, qui fugit ad illud
  Culmen, vbi pro te nemo dolere potest.

XXIV. *In Angelos*

INTELLECTVS adultus Angelorum
  Haud nostro similis, cui necesse,
  Vt dentur species, rogare sensum:
  Et ni lumina ianuam resignent,
  Et nostrae tribuant molae farinam,
  Saepe ex se nihil otiosa cudit.
  A nobis etenim procul remoti
  Labuntur fluuij scientiarum:
  Si non per species, nequimus ipsi,
  Quid ipsi sumus, assequi putando.
  Non tantum est iter Angelis ad vndas,
  Nullo circuitu scienda pungunt,
  Illis perpetuae patent fenestrae,
  Se per se facili modo scientes,
  Atque ipsi sibi sunt mola & farina.

XXV. *Roma. Anagr.*   { Oram. Maro.
{ Ramo. Armo.
{ Mora. Amor.

ROMA, tuum nomen quam non pertransijt ORAM,
    Cùm Latium ferrent secula prisca iugum?
Non deerat vel fama tibi, vel carmina famae,
    Vnde MARO laudes duxit ad astra tuas.
At nunc exucco similis tua gloria RAMO
    A veteri trunco & nobilitate cadit.
Laus antiqua & honor perijt: quasi scilicet ARMO
    Te deiecissent tempora longa suo.
Quin tibi tam desperatae MORA nulla medetur,
    Quâ Fabio quondam sub duce nata salus.
Hinc te olim gentes mirate odere vicissim;
    Et cum sublatâ laude recedit AMOR.

XXVI. *Vrbani VIII Pont. Respons.*

CVM Romam nequeas, quod aues, euertere, nomen
    Inuertis, mores carpis & obloqueris:
Te Germana tamen pubes, te Graecus & Anglus
    Arguit, exceptos quos pia Roma fouet:
Hostibus haec etiam parcens imitatur Iesum.
    Inuertis nomen. Quid tibi dicit? AMOR.

XXVII. *Respons. ad Vrb. VIII*

NON placet vrbanus noster de nomine lusus
    Romano, sed res seria Roma tibi est:
Nempe Caput Romae es, cuius mysteria velles
    Esse iocum soli, plebe stupente, tibi:
Attamen VRBANI delecto nomine, constat
    Quàm satur & suauis sit tibi Roma iocus.

XXVIII. *Ad Vrbanum VIII Pont.*

PONTIFICEM tandem nacta est sibi Roma poetam:
  Res redit ad vates, Pieriósque duces:
Quod Bellarminus nequijt, fortasse poetae
  Suauiter efficient, absque rigore Scholae.
Cedito Barbaries: Helicon iam litibus instat,
  Squalorémque togae candida Musa fugat.

XXIX. *Λογικὴ Θυσία*

ARARÚMQVE Hominúmque ortum si mente pererres,
  Cespes viuus, Homo; mortuus, Ara fuit:
Quae diuisa nocent, Christi per foedus, in vnum
  Conueniunt; & Homo viua fit Ara Dei.

XXX. *In Thomam Didymum*

DVM te vel digitis minister vrget,
Et hoc indicium subis, Redemptor?
Nempe es totus amor, medulla amoris,
Qui spissae fidei breuíque menti
Paras hospitium torúmque dulcem,
Quô se condat & implicet volutans
Ceu fidâ statione & arce certâ,
Ne perdat Leo rugiens vagantem.

XXXI. *In Solarium*

CONIVGIVM Caeli Terraéque haec machina praestat;
  Debetur Caelo lumen, & vmbra solo:

Sic Hominis moles animâque & corpore constat,
　　Cuius ab oppositis fluxit origo locis.
Contemplare, miser, quantum terroris haberet
　　Vel sine luce solum, vel sine mente caro.

XXXII. *Triumphus Mortis*

O MEA suspicienda manus, ventérque perennis!
Quem non Emathius torrens, non sanguine pinguis
Daunia, non satiat bis ter millesima caedis
Progenies, mundíque aetas abdomine nostro
Ingluuiéque minor. Quercus habitare feruntur
Prisci, crescentésque vnà cum prole cauernas:
Nec tamen excludor: namque vnâ ex arbore vitam
Glans dedit, & truncus tectum, & ramalia mortem.
　　Confluere intereà passim ad Floralia pubes
Coeperat, agricolis mentémque & aratra solutis:
Compita feruescunt pedibus, clamoribus aether.
Hìc vbi discumbunt per gramina, salsior vnus
Omnia suspendit naso, sociósque lacessit:
Non fert Vcalegon, atque amentata retorquet
Dicta ferox: haerent lateri conuitia fixo.
Scinditur in partes vulgus ceu compita: telum
Ira facit, mundúsque ipse est apotheca furoris.
Liber alit rixas: potantibus omnia bina
Sunt, praeter vitam: saxis hic sternitur, alter
Ambustis sudibus: pars vitam in pocula fundunt,
In patinas alij: furit inconstantia vini
Sanguine, quem dederat, spolians. Primordia Mortis
Haec fuerant: sic Tisiphone virguncula lusit.
　　Non placuit rudis atque ignara occisio: Morti
Quaeritur ingenium, doctúsque homicida probatur.
Hinc tyrocinium, paruóque assueta iuuentus,

Fictáque Bellona & verae ludibria pugnae,
Instructaéque acies, hyemésque in pellibus actae,
Omniáque haec vt transadigant sine crimine costas,
Artificésque necis clueant, & mortis alumni.
Nempe & millenos ad palum interficit hostes
Assiduus tyro, si sit spectanda voluntas.
Heu miseri! Quis tantùm ipsis virtutibus instat
Quantùm caedi? adeón' vnam vos pascere vitam,
Perdere sexcentas? crescit tamen hydra nocendi
Tristis, vbi ac ferrum tellure reciditur imâ,
Faecundúsque chalybs sceleris, iam sanguine tinctus,
Expleri nequit, & totum depascitur Orbem.
Quid memorem tormenta, quibus prius horruit aeuum;
Balistásque Onagrósque & quicquid Scorpio saeuus
Vel Catapulta potest, Siculíque inuenta magistri,
Anglorúmque arcus gaudentes sanguine Galli,
Fustibalos fundásque, quibus, cum Numine, fretus
Strauit Idumaeum diuinus Tityrus hostem?
Adde etiam currus, & cum temone Britanno
Aruiragum, falcésque obstantia quaeque metentes.
Quin Aries ruit, & multâ Demetrius arte:
Sic olim cecidere.
    Deerat adhuc vitijs hominum dignissima mundo
Machina, quam nullum satìs execrabitur aeuum;
Liquitur ardenti candens fornace metallum,
Fusáque decurrit notis aqua ferrea sulcis:
Exoritur tubus, atque instar Cyclopis Homeri
Luscum prodigium, medióque foramine gaudens.
Inde rotae atque axes subeunt, quasi sella curulis
Quâ Mors ipsa sedens hominum de gente triumphat.
Accedit Pyrius puluis, laquearibus Orci
Erutus, infernae pretiosa tragemata mensae,
Sulphureóque lacu, totáque imbuta Mephiti.
Huic Glans adijcitur (non quam ructare vetustas
Creditur, ante satas prono cum numine fruges)

Plumbea glans, liuensque suae quasi conscia noxae,
Purpureus lictor Plutonis, epistola Fati
Plumbis obsignata, colósque & stamina vitae
Perrumpens, Atropi vetulae marcentibus vlnis.

Haec vbi iuncta, subit viuo cum fune minister,
Fatalémque leuans dextram, quâ stupeus ignis
Mulcetur vento, accendit cum fomite partem
Pulueris inferni; properat datus ignis, & omnem
Materiam vexat: nec iam se continet antro
Tisiphone; flammâ & fallaci fulmine cincta
Euolat, horrendúmque ciet bacchata fragorem.
It stridor, caelósque omnes & Tartara findit.
Non iam exaudiri quicquam vel Musica caeli
Vel gemitus Erebi: piceo se turbine voluens
Totámque eructans nubem, Glans proruit imo
Praecipitata; cadunt vrbes, formidine muri
Diffugiunt, fragilísque crepant coenacula mundi.
Strata iacent toto millena cadauera campo
Vno ictu: non sic pestis, non stella maligno
Afflatu perimunt: en, Cymba Cocytia turbis
Ingemit, & defessus opem iam Portitor orat.
Nec Glans sola nocet; mortem quandoque susurrat
Aura volans, vitámque aer, quam pauerat, aufert.

Dicite, vos Furiae, quâ gaudet origine Monstrum.
Nox Aetnam, noctémque Chaos genuere priores.
Aetna Cacum igniuomum dedit, hic Ixiona multis
Cantatum; deinde Ixion cum nubibus atris
Congrediens genuit Monachum, qui limen opacae
Triste colens cellae, noctúque & Daemone plenum,
Protulit horrendum hoc primus cum puluere monstrum.
Quis Monachos mortem meditari, & puluere tristi
Versatos neget, atque humiles, queîs talia cordi
Tam demissa, ipsámque adeò subeuntia terram?

Nec tamen hîc noster stetit impetus: exilit omni
Tormento peior Iesuita, & fulminat Orbem,

Ridens Bombardas miseras, quae corpora perdunt
Non animas, raróque ornantur sanguine regum
Obstreperae stulto sonitu, criménque fatentes.
Imperij hìc culmen figo: mortalibus actum est
Corporéque atque animo. Totus mihi seruiat Orbis.

XXXIII. *Triumphus Christiana. In Mortem*

Ain' verò? quanta praedicas? hercle aedepol,
Magnificus es screator, homicida inclytus.
Quid ipse faciam? qui nec arboreas sudes
In te, nec arcus, scorpionésue, aut rotas,
Gladiósue, Catapultásue teneam, quin neque
Alapas nec Arietes? Quid ergo? Agnum & Crucem.

XXXIV. *In Johannem* ἐπιστήθιον

Ah nunc, helluo, fac, vt ipse sugam:
Num totum tibi pectus imputabis?
Fontem intercipis omnibus patentem?
Quin pro me quoque sanguinem profudit,
Et ius pectoris inde consecutus
Lac cum sanguine posco deuolutum;
Vt, si gratia tanta copuletur
Peccati veniae mei, vel ipsos
Occumbens humero Thronos lacessam.

XXXV. *Ad Dominum*

Christe, decus, dulcedo, & centum circiter Hyblae,
Cordis apex, animae pugnáque páxque meae,
Quin, sine, te cernam; quoties iam dixero, cernam;
Immoriárque oculis, o mea vita, tuis.

Si licet, immoriar: vel si tua visio vita est,
    Cur sine te, votis immoriturus, ago?
Ah, cernam; Tu, qui caecos sanare solebas,
    Cùm te non videam, méne videre putas?
Non video, certum est iurare; aut si hoc vetuisti,
    Praeuenias vultu non facienda tuo.

FINIS

Soli Deo Gloria.

MEMORIAE MATRIS SACRVM

I

A h Mater, quo te deplorem fonte? Dolores
    Quae guttae poterunt enumerare meos?
Sicca meis lacrymis Thamesis vicina videtur,
    Virtutúmque choro siccior ipse tuo.
In flumen moerore nigrum si funderer ardens,
    Laudibus haud fierem sepia iusta tuis.
Tantùm istaec scribo gratus, ne tu mihi tantùm
    Mater: & ista Dolor nunc tibi Metra parit.

II

C orneliae sanctae, graues Semproniae,
Et quicquid vspiam est seuerae foeminae,
Conferte lacrymas: Illa, quae vos miscuit
Vestrásque laudes, poscit & mixtas genas.
Namque hanc ruinam salua Grauitas defleat,
Pudórque constet vel solutis crinibus;
Quandoque vultûs sola maiestas, Dolor.
   Decus mulierum perijt: & metuunt viri
Vtrumque sexum dote ne mulctauerit.
Non illa soles terere comptu lubricos,
Struices superbas atque turritum caput
Molita, reliquum deinde garriens diem
(Nam post Babelem linguae adest confusio)
Quin post modestam, qualis integras decet,
Substructionem capitis & nimbum breuem,
Animam recentem rite curauit sacris
Adorta numen acri & igneâ prece.
   Dein familiam lustrat, & res prandij,

Horti, colíque distributim pensitat.
Suum cuique tempus & locus datur.
Inde exiguntur pensa crudo vespere.
Ratione certâ vita constat & domus,
Prudenter inito quot diebus calculo.
Totâ renident aede decus & suauitas
Animo renidentes priùs. Sin rarior
Magnatis appulsu extulit se occasio,
Surrexit vnà & illa, seséque extulit:
Occasione certat, imò & obtinet.
Proh! quantus imber, quanta labri comitas,
Lepos seuerus, Pallas mixta Gratijs;
Loquitur numellas, compedes & retia:
Aut si negotio hora sumenda est, rei
Per angiportus & maeandros labitur,
Ipsos Catones prouocans oraculis.
Tum quanta tabulis artifex? quae scriptio?
Bellum putamen, nucleus bellissimus,
Sententiae cum voce mirè conuenit,
Volant per orbem literae notissimae:
O blanda dextra, neutiquam istoc pulueris,
Quò nunc recumbis, scriptio merita est tua,
Pactoli arena tibi tumulus est vnicus.
   Adde his trientem Musices, quae molliens
Mulcénsque dotes caeteras visa est quasi
Caelestis harmoniae breue praeludium.
Quàm mira tandem Subleuatrix pauperum!
Languentium baculus, teges iacentium,
Commune cordis palpitantis balsamum:
Benedictiones publicae cingunt caput,
Caelíque referunt & praeoccupant modum.
Fatisco referens tanta quae numerant mei
Solùm dolores, & dolores, stellulae.
   At tu qui ineptè haec dicta censes filio,
Nato parentis auferens Encomium,

Abito, trunce, cum tuis pudoribus.
Ergo ipse solùm mutus atque excors ero
Strepente mundo tinnulis praeconijs?
Mihíne matris vrna clausa est vnico,
Herbae exoletae, ros-marinus aridus?
Matríne linguam refero, solùm vt mordeam?
Abito, barde. Quàm piè istic sum impudens!
Tu verò mater perpetim laudabere
Nato dolenti: literae hoc debent tibi
Queîs me educasti; sponte chartas illinunt
Fructum laborum consecutae maximum
Laudando Matrem, cùm repugnant inscij.

III

Cvr splendes, O Phoebe? ecquid demittere matrem
  Ad nos cum radio tam rutilante potes?
At superat caput illa tuum, quantum ipsa cadauer
  Mens superat; corpus solùm Elementa tenent.
Scilicet id splendes: haec est tibi causa micandi,
  Et lucro apponis gaudia sancta tuo.
Verùm heus, si nequeas caelo demittere matrem,
  Sítque omnis motûs nescia tanta quies,
Fac radios saltem ingemines, vt dextera tortos
  Implicet, & matrem, matre manente, petam.

IV

  Qvid nugor calamo fauens?
Mater perpetuis vuida gaudijs,
  Horto pro tenui colit
Edenem Boreae flatibus inuium.
  Quin caeli mihi sunt mei,
Materni decus, & debita nominis,
  Dúmque his inuigilo frequens
Stellarum socius, pellibus exuor.

Quare Sphaerem egomet meam
Connixus, digitis impiger vrgeo:
　　Te, Mater, celebrans diu,
　　　Noctu te celebrans luminis aemulo.

　　Per te nascor in hunc globum
Exemplóque tuo nascor in alterum:
　　Bis tu mater eras mihi,
　　　Vt currat paribus gloria tibijs.

V

HORTI, deliciae *Dominae*, marcescite tandem;
　　Ornâstis capulum, nec superesse licet.
Ecce decus vestrum spinis horrescit, acutâ
　　Cultricem reuocans anxietate manum:
Terram & funus olent flores: Dominaéque cadauer
　　Contiguas stirpes afflat, eaéque rosas.
In terram violae capite inclinantur opaco,
　　Quaéque domus Dominae sit, grauitate docent.
Quare haud vos hortos, sed coemeteria dico,
　　Dum torus absentem quisque reponit heram.
Eugè, perite omnes; nec posthâc exeat vlla
　　Quaesitum Dominam gemma vel herba suam.
Cuncta ad radices redeant, tumulósque paternos;
　　(Nempe sepulcra Satis numen inempta dedit.)
Occidite; aut sanè tantisper viuite, donec
　　Vespere ros maestis funus honestet aquis.

VI

GALENE, frustra es, cur miserum premens
Tot quaestionum fluctibus obruis,
　　Arterias tractans micantes
　　　Corporeae fluidaéque molis?

Aegroto mentis: quam neque pixides
Nec tarda possunt pharmaca consequi,
  Vtrumque si praederis Indum,
    Vltrà animus spatiatur exlex.
Impos medendi, occidere si potes,
Nec si parentem ducar ad optimam:
  Ni sanctè, vti mater, recedam,
    Morte magìs viduabor illâ.
Quin cerne vt erres, inscie, brachium
Tentando sanum: si calet, aestuans,
  Ardore scribendi calescit,
    Mater inest saliente venâ.
Si totus infler, si tumeam crepax,
Ne membra culpes, causa animo latet
  Qui parturit laudes parentis:
    Nec grauidis medicina tuta est.
Irregularis nunc habitus mihi est:
Non exigatur crasis ad alterum:
  Quod tu febrem censes, salubre est
    Atque animo medicatur vnum.

VII

Pallida materni Genij atque exanguis imago,
In nebulas similésque tui res gaudia nunquid
Mutata? & pro matre mihi phantasma dolosum
Vberáque aerea hiscentem fallentia natum?
Vae nubi pluuiâ grauidae, non lacte, meásque
Ridenti lacrymas quibus vnis concolor vnda est.
Quin fugias? mea non fuerat tam nubila Iuno,
Tam segnis facies aurorae nescia vernae,
Tam languens genitrix cineri supposta fugaci:
Verùm augusta parens, sanctum os caelóque locandum,

Quale paludosos iamiam lictura recessus
Praetulit Astraea, aut solio Themis alma vetusto
Pensilis, atque acri dirimens Examine lites.
Hunc vultum ostendes, & tecum, nobile spectrum,
Quod superest vitae, insumam: Solísque iugales
Ipse tuae solùm adnectam, sine murmure, thensae.
Nec querar ingratos, studijs dum tabidus insto,
Effluxisse dies, suffocatámue Mineruam,
Aut spes productas, barbatáque somnia vertam
In vicium mundo sterili, cui cedo cometas
Ipse suos tanquam digno pallentiáque astra.

   Est mihi bis quinis laqueata domuncula tignis
Rure; breuísque hortus, cuius cum vellere florum
Luctatur spacium, qualem tamen eligit aequi
Iudicij dominus, flores vt iunctiùs halent
Stipati, rudibúsque volis imperuius hortus
Sit quasi fasciculus crescens, & nidus odorum.
Hîc ego túque erimus, variae suffitibus herbae
Quotidie pasti: tantùm verum indue vultum
Affectûsque mei similem; nec languida misce
Ora meae memori menti: ne dispare cultu
Pugnaces, teneros florum turbemus odores,
Atque inter reliquos horti crescentia foetus
Nostra etiam paribus marcescant gaudia fatis.

VIII

PARVAM piámque dum lubenter semitam
   Grandi reaéque praefero,
Carpsit malignum sydus hanc modestiam
   Vinúmque felle miscuit.
Hinc fremere totus & minari gestio
   Ipsis seuerus orbibus;

Tandem prehensâ comiter lacernulâ
    Susurrat aure quispiam,
Haec fuerat olim potio Domini tui.
    Gusto probóque Dolium.

IX

Hoc, Genitrix, scriptum proles tibi sedula mittit.
    Siste parum cantus, dum legis ista, tuos.
Nôsse sui quid agant, quaedam est quoque musica sanctis,
    Quaéque olim fuerat cura, manere potest.
Nos miserè flemus, solésque obducimus almos
    Occiduis, tanquam duplice nube, genis.
Interea classem magnis Rex instruit ausis:
    Nos autem flemus: res ea sola tuis.
Ecce solutura est, ventos causata morantes:
    Sin pluuiam, fletus suppeditâsset aquas.
Tillius incumbit Dano, Gallúsque marinis,
    Nos flendo: haec nostrûm tessera sola ducum.
Sic aeuum exigitur tardum, dum praepetis anni
    Mille rotae nimijs impediuntur aquis.
Plura tibi missurus eram (nam quae mihi laurus,
    Quod nectar, nisi cum te celebrare diem?)
Sed partem in scriptis etiam dum lacryma poscit,
    Diluit oppositas candidus humor aquas.

X

Nempe huc vsque notos tenebricosos
Et maestum nimio madore Caelum
Tellurísque Britannicae saliuam
Iniustè satìs arguit viator.
At te commoriente, Magna Mater,
Rectè, quem trahit, aerem repellit

Cum probro madidum, reúmque difflat.
Nam te nunc Ager, Vrbs, & Aula plorant:
Te nunc Anglia, Scotiaéque binae,
Quin te Cambria peruetusta deflet,
Deducens lacrymas prioris aeui
Ne serae meritis tuis venirent.
Non est angulus vspiam serenus,
Nec cingit mare, nunc inundat omnes.

XI

Dvm librata suis haeret radicibus ilex
   Nescia vulturnis cedere, firma manet.
Post vbi crudelem sentit diuisa securem,
   Quò placet oblato, mortua fertur, hero:
Arbor & ipse inuersa vocer: dúmque insitus almae
   Assideo Matri, robore vinco cedros.
Nunc sorti pateo, expositus sine matre procellis,
   Lubricus, & superans mobilitate salum.
Tu radix, tu petra mihi firmissima, Mater,
   Ceu Polypus, chelis saxa prehendo tenax:
Non tibi nunc soli filum abrupere sorores,
   Dissutus videor funere & ipse tuo.
Vnde vagans passim rectè vocer alter Vlysses,
   Alteráque haec tua mors, Ilias esto mihi.

XII

Facesse, Stoica plebs, obambulans cautes,
Exuta strato carnis, ossibus constans,
Iísque siccis adeò vt os Molossorum
Haud glubat inde tres teruncios escae.
Dolere prohibes? aut dolere me gentis
Adeò inficetae, plumbeae, Meduseae,

Ad saxa speciem retrahentis humanam,
Tantóque nequioris optimâ Pirrhâ?
At fortè matrem perdere haud soles demens:
Quin nec potes; cui praebuit Tigris partum.
Proinde parco belluis, nec irascor.

XIII

EPITAPHIVM

HIC sita foeminei laus & victoria sexus:
Virgo pudens, vxor fida, seuera parens:
Magnatúmque inopúmque aequum certamen & ardor:
Nobilitate illos, hos pietate rapit.
Sic excelsa humilísque simul loca dissita iunxit,
Quicquid habet tellus, quicquid & astra, fruens.

XIV

Ψυχῆς ἀσθενὲς ἕρκος, ἀμαυρὸν πνεύματος ἄγγος,
Τῷδε παρὰ τύμβῳ δίζεο, φίλε, μόνον.
Νοῦ δ' αὐτοῦ τάφος ἐστ' ἀστήρ· φέγγος γὰρ ἐκείνου
Φεγγώδη μόνον, ὡς εἰκός, ἔπαυλιν ἔχει.
Νῦν ὁράας, ὅτι κάλλος ἀπείριτον ὠπὸς ἀπαυγοῦς
Οὐ σαθρόν, οὐδὲ μελῶν ἔπλετο, ἀλλὰ νόος·
Ὃς διὰ σωματίου πρότερον καὶ νῦν δι' Ὀλύμπου
Ἀστράπτων, θυρίδων ὡς δία, νεῖμε σέλας.

XV

Μῆτερ, γυναικῶν αἴγλη, ἀνθρώπων ἔρις,
Ὄδυρμα Δαιμόνων, Θεοῦ γεώργιον,
Πῶς νῦν ἀφίπτασαι, γόου καὶ κινδύνου
Ἡμᾶς λιποῦσα κυκλόθεν μεταιχμίους;
Μενοῦνγε σοφίην, εἰ σ' ἀπηλλάχθαι χρεών,

Ζωῆς ξυνεργὸν τήνδε διαθεῖναι τέκνοις
Ἐχρῆν φυγοῦσα, τήν τ' ἐπιστήμην βίου.
Μενοῦν τὸ γλαφυρόν, καὶ μελίρροον τρόπων,
Λόγων τε φίλτρον, ὥσθ' ὑπεξελθεῖν λεών.
Νῦν δ' ὤχου ἔνθενδ' ὡς στρατὸς νικηφόρος
Φέρων τὸ πᾶν, κἀγων· ἢ ὡς Ἀπαρκτίας
Κήπου συνωθῶν ἀνθινὴν εὐωδίαν,
Μίαν τ' ἀταρπὸν συμπορεύεσθαι δράσας.
Ἐγὼ δὲ ῥινὶ ξυμβαλὼν ἰχνηλατῶ
Εἴ που τύχοιμι τῆσδ' ἀρίστης ἀτραποῦ,
Θανεῖν συνειδὼς κρεῖττον, ἢ ἄλλως βιοῦν.

XVI

Χαλεπὸν δοκεῖ δακρῦσαι,
Χαλεπὸν μὲν οὐ δακρῦσαι·
Χαλεπώτερον δὲ πάντων
Δακρύοντας ἀμπαύεσθαι.
Γενέτειραν οὔ τις ἀνδρῶν
Διδύμαις κόραις τοιαύτην
Ἐποδύρεται πρεπόντως.
Τάλας, εἴθε γ' Ἄργος εἴην
Πολυόμματος, πολύτλας,
Ἵνα μητρὸς εὐθενούσης
Ἀρετὰς διακριθείσας
Ἰδίαις κόραισι κλαύσω.

XVII

Αἰάζω γενέτειραν, ἐπαιάζουσι καὶ ἄλλοι,
Οὐκ ἔτ' ἐμὴν ἰδίας φυλῆς γράψαντες ἀρωγόν,
Προυνομίῳ δ' ἀρετῆς κοινὴν γενέτειραν ἑλόντες.
Οὐκ ἔνι θαῦμα τόσον σφετερίζειν· οὐδὲ γὰρ ὕδωρ,
Οὐ φέγγος, κοινόν τ' ἀγαθόν, μίαν εἰς θύραν εἴργειν

Ἦ θέμις, ἢ δυνατόν. σεμνώματος ἔπλετο στάθμη,
Δημόσιόν τ' ἴνδαλμα καλοῦ, θεῖόν τε κάτοπτρον.
   Αἰάζω γενέτειραν, ἐπαιάζουσι γυναῖκες,
Οὐκ ἔτι βαλλομένης χάρισιν βεβολημέναι ἦτορ,
Αὐτὰρ ἄχει μεγάλῳ κεντούμεναι· εὖτε γὰρ αὗται
Τῆς περὶ συλλαλέουσι, ἑοῦ ποικίλματος ἄρδην
Λήσμονες, ἡ βελόνη σφαλερῷ κῆρ τραύματι νύττει
Ἔργου ἁμαρτηκυῖα, νέον πέπλον αἵματι στικτὸν
Μητέρι τεκταίνουσα, γόῳ καὶ πένθεσι σύγχρουν.
   Αἰάζω γενέτειραν, ἐπαιάζουσιν ὀπῶραι,
Οὐκ ἔτι δεσποίνης γλυκερᾷ μελεδῶνι τραφεῖσαι·
Ἧς βίος ἠελίοιο δίκην, ἀκτῖνας ἱέντος
Πραεῖς εἰαρινούς τε χαραῖς ἐπικίδνατο κῆπον·
Αὐτὰρ ὅδ' αὖ θάνατος κυρίης, ὡς ἥλιος αὖος
Σειρίου ἡττηθεὶς βουλήμασι, πάντα μαραίνει.
Ζῶ δ' αὐτός, βραχύ τι πνείων, ὥστ' ἔμπαλιν αὐτῆς
Αἶνον ὁμοῦ ζώειν καὶ πνεύματος ἄλλο γενέσθαι
Πνεῦμα, βίου πάροδον μούνοις ἐπέεσσι μετρῆσαι.

XVIII

Κύματ' ἐπαφριοῶντα Θαμήσεος, αἴκε σελήνης
   Φωτὸς ἀπαυραμένης ὄγκου ἐφεῖσθε πλέον,
Νῦν θέμις ὀρφναίῃ μεγάλης ἐπὶ γείτονος αἴσῃ
   Οὐλυμπόνδε βιβᾶν ὔμμιν ἀνισταμένοις.
Ἀλλὰ μενεῖτ', οὐ γὰρ τάραχος ποτὶ μητέρα βαίνῃ,
   Καὶ πρέπον ὧδε παρὰ δακρυόεσσι ῥέειν.

XIX

Excvssos manibus calamos, falcémque resumptam
   Rure, sibi dixit Musa fuisse probro.
Aggreditur Matrem (conductis carmine Parcis)
   Funeréque hoc cultum vindicat aegra suum.

Non potui non ire acri stimulante flagello:
  Quin Matris superans carmina poscit honos.
Eia, agedum scribo: vicisti, Musa; sed audi,
  Stulta: semel scribo, perpetuò vt sileam.

ALIA POEMATA LATINA

In Obitum Henrici Principis Walliae

ITE leues (inquam), Parnassia numina, Musae,
Non ego vos posthâc hederae velatus amictu
Somnis (nescio queîs) nocturna ad vota vocabo:
Sed nec Cyrrhaei saltus Libethriáue arua
In mea dicta ruant; non tam mihi pendula mens est,
Sic quasi Dijs certem, magnos accersere montes:
Nec vaga de summo deducam flumina monte,
Qualia parturiente colunt sub rupe sorores:
Si quas mens agitet moles (dum pectora saeuo
Tota stupent luctu) lachrymísque exaestuet aequis
Spiritus, hi mihi iam montes, haec flumina sunto.
Musa, vale, & tu Phoebe; dolor mea carmina dictet;
Hinc mihi principium: vos o labentia mentis
Lumina, nutantes paulatim acquirite vires,
Viuite, dum mortem ostendam: sic tempora vestram
Non comedant famam, sic nulla obliuia potent.
Quare age, Mens, effare, precor, quo numine laeso?
Quae suberant causae? quid nos committere tantum,
Quod non Lanigerae pecudes, non Agmina lustrent?
Annon longa fames miseraéque iniuria pestis
Poena minor fuerat, quàm fatum Principis aegrum?
Iam foelix Philomela, & menti conscia Dido!
Foelices, quos bella premunt, & plurimus ensis!
Non metuunt vltrà; nostra infortunia tantùm
Fatáque Fortunásque & spem laesêre futuram.
Quòd si fata illi longam invidêre salutem
Et patrio regno (sub quo iam Principe nobis
Quid sperare, imò quid non sperare licebat?)
Debuit ista pati prima & non nobilis aetas:

Aut cita mors est danda bonis aut longa senectus:
Sic lactare animos & sic ostendere gemmam
Excitat optatus auidos, & ventilat ignem.
Quare etiam nuper Pyrij de pulueris ictu
Principis innocuam seruastis numina Vitam,
Vt morbi perimant, alióque in puluere prostet?
Phoebe, tui puduit quum summo manè redires
Sol sine sole tuo! quàm te tum nubibus atris
Totum offuscari peteres, vt nocte silenti
Humana aeternos agerent praecordia questus:
Tantùm etenim vestras (Parcae) non flectit habenas
Tempus edax rerum, túque o mors improba sola es,
Cui caecas tribuit vires annosa vetustas.
Quid non mutatum est? requiêrunt flumina cursus;
Plus etiam veteres coelum videre remotum:
Cur ideo verbis tristes effundere curas
Expeto, tanquam haec sit nostri medicina doloris?
Immodicus luctus tacito vorat igne medullas,
Vt, fluuio currente, vadum sonat, alta quiescunt.

INNVPTA Pallas, nata Diespitre,
Aeterna summae gloria regiae,
    Cui dulcis arrident Camoenae
      Pieridis Latiaéque Musae,

Cur tela Mortis vel tibi vel tuis
Quâcunque guttâ temporis imminent?
    Tantâque propendet staterâ
      Regula sanguinolenta fati?

Númne Hydra talis, tántáne bellua est
Mors tot virorum sordida sanguine,
    Vt mucro rumpatur Mineruae,
      Vtque minax superetur Aegis?

Tu flectis amnes, tu mare caerulum
Vssisse prono fulmine diceris,
　　Aiacis exesas triremes
　　　　Praecipitans grauiore casu.

Tu discidisti Gorgoneas manus
Nexas, capillos anguibus oblitos,
　　Furuósque vicisti Gigantes,
　　　　Enceladum pharetrámque Rhoeci.

Ceu victa, Musis porrigit herbulas
Pennata caeci dextra Cupidinis,
　　Non vlla Bellonae furentis
　　　　Arma tui metuunt alumni.

Pallas retortis caesia vocibus
Respondit: Eia, ne metuas, precor,
　　Nam fata non iustis repugnant
　　　　Principibus, sed amica fiunt.

Vt si recisis arboribus meis
Nudetur illic lucus amabilis,
　　Fructúsque post mortem recusent
　　　　Perpetuos mihi ferre rami,

Dulcem rependent tum mihi tibiam
Pulchrè renatam ex arbore mortuâ,
　　Dignámque coelesti coronâ
　　　　Harmoniam dabit inter astra.

　　　　　　　　G. Herbert Coll. Trin.

In Natales et Pascha Concurrentes

Cvm tu, Christe, cadis, nascor; mentémque ligauit
    Vna meam membris horula, téque cruci.
O me disparibus natum cum numine fatis!
    Cur mihi das vitam, quam tibi, Christe, negas?
Quin moriar tecum: vitam, quam negligis ipse,
    Accipe; ni talem des, tibi qualis erat.
Hoc mihi legatum tristi si funere praestes,
    Christe, duplex fiet mors tua vita mihi:
Atque vbi per te sanctificer natalibus ipsis,
    In vitam & neruos Pascha coaeua fluet.

In Obitum Serenissimae Reginae Annae

Qvo Te, foelix Anna, modo deflere licebit?
    Cui magnum imperium, gloria maior erat:
Ecce meus torpens animus succumbit vtrique,
    Cui tenuis fama est, ingeniúmque minus.
Quis, nisi qui manibus Briareus, oculísque sit Argus,
    Scribere, Te dignùm, vel lachrymare queat!
Frustra igitur sudo: superest mihi sola voluptas,
    Quòd calamum excusent Pontus & Astra meum:
Namque Annae laudes coelo scribuntur aperto,
    Sed luctus noster scribitur Oceano.
                       G. Herbert Coll. Trin. Soc.

Ad Autorem Instaurationis Magnae

Per strages licet autorum veterúmque ruinam
    Ad famae properes vera Tropaea tuae,
Tam nitidè tamen occidis, tam suauiter, hostes,
    Se quasi donatum funere quisque putat.

Scilicet apponit pretium tua dextera fato,
  Vulneréque emanat sanguis, vt intret honos.
O quàm felices sunt, qui tua castra sequuntur,
  Cùm per te sit res ambitiosa mori.

Comparatio inter Munus Summi Cancellariatus et Librum

Mvnere dum nobis prodes, Libróque futuris,
  In laudes abeunt secula quaeque tuas;
Munere dum nobis prodes, Libróque remotis,
  In laudes abeunt iam loca quaeque tuas:
Hae tibi sunt alae laudum. Cui contigit vnquam
  Longius aeterno, latius orbe decus?

In Honorem Illustr. D.D. Verulamij, S^{ti} Albani, Mag. Sigilli Custodis post editam ab eo Instaurationem Magnam

Qvis iste tandem? non enim vultu ambulat
Quotidiano! Nescis, ignare? Audies!
Dux Notionum; veritatis Pontifex;
Inductionis Dominus, & Verulamij;
Rerum magister vnicus, at non Artium;
Profunditatis pinus, atque Elegantiae;
Naturae Aruspex intimus; Philosophiae
Aerarium; sequester expèrientiae,
Speculationísque; Aequitatis signifer;
Scientiarum, sub pupillari statu
Degentium olim, Emancipator; Luminis
Promus; Fugator Idolûm, atque nubium;
Collega Solis; Quadra Certitudinis;

Sophismatomastix; Brutus Literarius,
Authoritatis exuens tyrannidem;
Rationis & sensûs stupendus Arbiter;
Repumicator mentis; Atlas Physicus,
Alcide succumbente Stagiritico;
Columba Noae, quae in vetustis artibus
Nullum locum requiémue cernens perstitit
Ad se suaéque matris Arcam regredi:
Subtilitatis Terebra; Temporis Nepos
Ex Veritate matre; Mellis alueus;
Mundíque & Animarum sacerdos vnicus;
Securis errorum; ínque Naturalibus
Granum Sinapis, acre Alijs, crescens sibi:
  O me probè lassum! Iuuate, Posteri!

G. HERBERT Orat. Pub. in
Acad. Cantab.

Aethiopissa ambit Cestum Diuersi Coloris Virum

Qvid mihi si facies nigra est? hoc, Ceste, colore
 Sunt etiam tenebrae, quas tamen optat amor.
Cernis vt exustâ semper sit fronte viator;
 Ah longum, quae te deperit, errat iter.
Si nigro sit terra solo, quis despicit aruum?
 Claude oculos, & erunt omnia nigra tibi:
Aut aperi, & cernes corpus quas proijcit vmbras;
 Hoc saltem officio fungar amore tui.
Cùm mihi sit facies fumus, quas pectore flammas
 Iamdudum tacitè delituisse putes?
Dure, negas? O fata mihi praesaga doloris,
 Quae mihi lugubres contribuere genas!

Dum petit Infantem

DVM petit Infantem Princeps, Grantámque Iacobus,
  Quisnam horum maior sit, dubitatur, amor.
Vincit more suo Noster: nam millibus Infans
  Non tot abest, quot nos Regis ab ingenio.

While Prince to Spaine, and King to Cambridge goes,
The question is, whose loue the greater showes:
Ours (like himselfe) o'recomes; for his wit's more
Remote from ours, then Spaine from Britains shoare.

In obitum incomparabilis Francisci Vicecomitis Sancti Albani, Baronis Verulamij

DVM longi lentíque gemis sub pondere morbi
  Atque haeret dubio tabida vita pede,
Quid voluit prudens Fatum, iam sentio tandem:
  Constat, *Aprile* vno te potuisse mori:
Vt *Flos* hinc lacrymis, illinc *Philomela* querelis,
  Deducant *linguae* funera sola tuae.

GEORGIVS HERBERT

In Sacram Anchoram Piscatoris G. Herbert

QVOD Crux nequibat fixa, Clavíque additi,
(Tenere Christum scilicet, ne ascenderet)
Tuíue Christum deuocans facundia
Vltra loquendi tempus; addit Anchora:
Nec hoc abundè est tibi, nisi certae Anchorae

275

Addas sigillum: nempe Symbolum suae
Tibi debet Vnda & Terra certitudinis.

Munde, fluas fugiásque licet, nos nostráque fixi:
    Deridet motus sancta catena tuos.
    Quondam fessus Amor loquens Amato,
    Tot & tanta loquens amica, scripsit:
    Tandem & fessa manus, dedit sigillum.

Suauis erat, qui scripta dolens lacerando recludi,
Sanctius in Regno Magni credebat Amoris
(In quo fas nihil est rumpi) donare sigillum.

ALTHOUGH the Crosse could not Christ here detain,
Though nail'd unto't, but he ascends again,
Nor yet thy eloquence here keep him still,
But onely while thou speak'st; This Anchor will.
Nor canst thou be content, unlesse thou to
This certain Anchor adde a Seal, and so
The Water, and the Earth both unto thee
Doe owe the symbole of their certainty.
Let the world reel, we and all ours stand sure,
This holy Cable's of all storms secure.

    When Love being weary made an end
    Of kinde Expressions to his friend,
    He writ; when's hand could write no more,
    He gave the Seale, and so left o're.

How sweet a friend was he, who being griev'd
His letters were broke rudely up, believ'd
'Twas more secure in great Loves Common-weal
(Where nothing should be broke) to adde a Seal.

Another version

WHEN my dear Friend could write no more,
He gave this *Seal*, and, so gave ore.

When winds and waves rise highest, I am sure,
This *Anchor* keeps my *faith*, that, me secure.

APPENDIX

PRO SVPPLICI EVANGELICORVM MINISTRORVM IN ANGLIA

Ad Serenissimum Regem
contra Larvatam geminae Academiae Gorgonem Apologia,
sive Anti-tami-cami-categoria,
Authore *A.M.*

Responsum non dictum.

INSOLENS, audax, facinus nefandum,
Scillicet, poscit ratio ut decori,
Poscit ex omni officio ut sibi mens
    Conscia recti
Anxiam Christi vigilemque curam,
Quae pias terris animas relictis
Sublevans deducit in astra, nigroque
    Invidet Orco,
De sacri castâ ratione cultus,
De sacrosancti officij decoro
Supplicem ritu veteri libellum
    Porgere Regi,
Simplici mente atque animo integello,
Spiritu recto, et studijs modestis,
Numinis sancti veniam, et benigni
    Regis honorem
Rite praefantem: Scelus expiandum
Scilicet taurorum, ovium, suumque
Millibus centum, voluisse nudo
    Tangere verbo

Praesulum fastus: monuisse ritus
Impios, deridiculos, ineptos,
Lege, ceu labes maculasque, lectâ ex
       Gente fugandos.

Iusque-jurandum ingemuisse jura
Exigi contra omnia; tum misellis
Mentibus tristem laqueum inijci per
       Fasque nefasque.

Turbida illimi crucis in lavacro
Signa consignem? magico rotatu
Verba devolvam? sacra vox sacratâ im-
       murmuret undâ

Strigis in morem? Rationis usu ad-
fabor infantem vacuum? canoras
Ingeram nugas minus audienti
       Dicta puello?

Parvulo impostis manibus sacrabo
Gratiae foedus? Digitone sponsae
Annulus sponsi impositus sacrabit
       Connubiale

Foedus aeternae bonitatis? Vndâ
Num salutari mulier sacerdos
Tinget in vitam, Sephoramque reddet
       Lustrica mater?

Pilei quadrum capiti rotundo
Rite quadrabit? Pharium Camillo
Supparum Christi, et decus Antichristi
       Pontificale?

Pastor examen gregis exigendum
Curet invitus, celebrare coenam
Promptus arcanam, memorando Iesu
       Vulnera dira?

Cantibus certent Berecinthia aera
Musicum fractis, reboentve rauco
Templa mugitu? Illecebris supremi ah
      Rector Olympi

Captus humanis? libitumque nobis,
Scilicet, Regi id Superûm adlubescet?
Somniumque aegri cerebri profanum est
      Dictio sacra?

Haud secus lustri lupa Vaticani
Romuli faecem bibit, et bibendam
Porrigit poc'lo populisque et ipsis
      Regibus aureo.

Non ita aeterni Wittakerus acer
Luminis vindex patriaeque lumen
Dixit aut sensit: neque celsa summi
      Penna Renoldi,

Certa sublimes aperire calles,
Sueta coelestes iterare cursus,
Laeta misceri niveis beatae
      Civibus aulae:

Nec Tami aut Cami accola saniore
Mente, qui coelum sapit in frequenti
Hermathenaeo et celebri Lycaeo
      Culta juventus;

Cujus affulget Genio Iovae lux:
Cui nitens Sol justitiae renidet:
Quem jubar Christi radiantis alto
      Spectat Olympo.

Bucerum laudem, an memorabo magnum
Martyrem? Gemmas geminas renati
Aurei saecli, duo dura sacri
      Fulmina belli.

Alterum Camus liquido recursu,
Alterum Tamus trepidante lymphâ
Audijt, multum stupuitque magno
      Ore sonantem.

Anne mulcentem Rhodanum et Lemannum
Praedicem Bezam, viridi in senectâ?
Octies cujus trepidavit aetas
      Claudere denos

Solis anfractus reditusque, et ultra
Quinque percurrens spatiosa in annos
Longius florem viridantis aevi
      Prorogat et ver.

Oris erumpit scatebrâ perenni
Amnis exundans, gravidique rores
Gratiâ foecundâ animos apertis
      Auribus implent.

Major hic omni invidiâ, et superstes
Millibus mille, et Sadeele, et omnium
Maximo Calvino, alijsque veri
      Testibus aequis;

Voce olorinâ liquidas ad undas
Nunc canit laudes Genitoris almi,
Carmen et Nato canit eliquante
      Numinia aurâ,

Sensa de castu sacra puriore,
Dicta de cultu potiore sancta,
Arma quae in castris jugulent severi
      Tramitis hostes.

Cana cantanti juga ninguidarum
Alpium applaudunt, resonantque valles:
IVRA concentu nemorum sonoro
      Et pater Ister

Consonant longe: pater et bicornis
Rhenus assensum ingeminat: Garumna,
Sequana, atque Arar, Liger: insularum et
　　　　　Vndipotentum

Magna pars intenta Britannicarum
Voce conspirat liquidâ: solumque,
Et salum, et coelum, aemula praecinentis
　　　　　More modoque

Concinunt Bezae numeris modisque
Et polo plaudunt: referuntque leges
Lege quas sanxit pius ardor et Rex
　　　　　Scotobritannus.

Sicut edictum in tabulis ahenis
Servat aeternum pia cura Regis,
Qui mare et terras varijsque mundum
　　　　　Temperat horis:

Cujus aequalis Soboles Parenti
Gentis electae Pater atque Custos:
Par et ambobus veniens utrinque
　　　　　Spiritus almus.

Quippe Tres-unus Deus; unus Actus,
Vna natura est tribus; una virtus,
Vna majestas, Deitas et una,
　　　　　Gloria et una.

Vna vis immensa, perennis una
Vita, lux una, et sapientia una,
Vna mens, una et ratio, una vox et
　　　　　Vna voluntas,

Lenis, indulgens, facilis, benigna;
Dura et inclemens, rigida et severa;
Semper aeterna, omnipotens et aequa,
　　　　　Semper et alma:

Lucidum cujus speculum est, reflectens
Aureum vultus jubar et verendum,
Virginis proles sata coelo, et alti in-
　　　　terpres Olympi:

Qui Patris mentemque animumque sancti
Filius pandit face noctilucâ,
Sive doctrinae documenta, seu com-
　　　　pendia vitae.

Publicae, privae, sacra scita Regni
Regis ad nutum referens, domusque
Ad voluntatem Domini instituta
　　　　Singula librans,

Luce quam Phoebus melior refundit,
Lege quam legum tulit ipse lator,
Cujus exacti officij suprema est
　　　　Norma voluntas.

Caeca mens humana, hominum voluntas
Prava, et affectus rabidi: indigetque
Luce mens, normâ officij voluntas,
　　　　Lege libido.

Quisquis hanc surdâ negat aure, et orbâ
Mente dat ferri rapidis procellis,
Ter quater caudex, stolidusque et omni ex
　　　　Parte misellus.

Quisquis hanc pronâ bibit aure, quâ se
Fundit ubertim liquidas sub auras,
Ille ter prudens, sapiensque et omni ex
　　　　Parte beatus.

Ergo vos Cami proceres, Tamique,
Quos viâ flexit malesuadus error,
Denuo rectum, duce Rege Regum, in-
　　　　sistite callem.

Vos metus tangit si hominum nec ullus,
At Deum fandi memorem et nefandi
Vindicem sperate, et amoena solis
      Tartara Diris:

Quae manent sontes animas, trucesque
Praesulum fastus; male quos perurit
Pervigil zelus vigilum, et gregis cus-
      todia pernox,

Veste bis tinctâ Tyrio superbos
Murice, et pastos dape pinguiore
Regiâ quondam aut Saliari iniunctâ ab-
      domine coenâ.

Qualis Vrsini Damasique fastus
Turgidus, luxuque ferox, feroque
Ambitu pugnax, sacram et aedem et urbem
      Caede nefandâ

Civium incestavit, et ominosum
Traxit exemplum veniens in aevum
Praesulum quod nobilium indecorus
      Provocat ordo.

Quid fames auri sacra? quid cupido
Ambitus diri fera non propagat
Posteris culpae? mala damna quanta
      Plurima fundit?

REPRINTED LITHOGRAPHICALLY IN GREAT BRITAIN
AT THE UNIVERSITY PRESS, OXFORD
BY VIVIAN RIDLER
PRINTER TO THE UNIVERSITY